The
Experience
of
HOPE

Mission and Ministry
in Changing Urban Communities

Edited by
WAYNE STUMME

Augsburg ■ Minneapolis

THE EXPERIENCE OF HOPE
Mission and Ministry in Changing Urban Communities

Cover design: Lecy Design

Library of Congress Cataloging-in-Publication Data

The experience of hope : mission and ministry in changing urban
    communities / edited by Wayne Stumme.
        p.   cm.
    Includes bibliographical references.
    ISBN 0-8066-2546-5 (alk. paper)
        1. City churches—United States.   2. Pastoral theology—Lutheran
Church.   3. Lutheran Church—Membership.   I. Stumme, Wayne, 1929-

BV637.E96   1991
253'.0973'091732—dc20   91-8467
                                                                                          CIP

The paper used in this publication meets the minimum requirements of American National Standard for Information Sciences—Permanence of Paper for Printed Library Materials, ANSI Z329.48-1984.   ∞™

Manufactured in the U.S.A.   AF 9-2546

95   94   93   92   91   1   2   3   4   5   6   7   8   9   10

Contents

Part THREE: Emboldened by Hope: the Future of Lutheran Mission and Ministry in Changing Urban Communities

Contributors

Dr. James A. Bergquist, Pastor
Lutheran Church of the Good Shepherd
Moorhead, Minnesota
    Former Executive Director
    Division for Outreach
    Evangelical Lutheran Church in America

The Rev. Robert S. Hoyt
Director for Program, New Congregations, and Area Ministry
Division for Outreach
Evangelical Lutheran Church in America
Chicago, Illinois

The Rev. James J. Lobdell, Pastor
Holy Trinity Lutheran Church
Inglewood, California

Dr. John Milbrath, Pastor
East Koshkonong Lutheran Church
Cambridge, Wisconsin
    Former Urban Outreach Ministry Specialist
    Bethany Lutheran Church
    Portland, Oregon

Dr. Mary Nelson, President
Bethel New Life
Chicago, Illinois

The Rev. David T. Nelson, Pastor
Bethel Lutheran Church
Chicago, Illinois

The Rev. Heidi Neumark, Pastor
Transfiguration Lutheran Church
Bronx, New York

The Rev. Harvey S. Peters, Jr., Senior Pastor
Luther Memorial Lutheran Church
Madison, Wisconsin
    Former Associate Director
    Division for Mission in North America
    Lutheran Church in America

The Rev. Edward A. Ruen, Director
Next Door Foundation
Our Savior's Lutheran Church
Milwaukee, Wisconsin

Dr. Harold D. Schlactenhaufen, Campus Pastor
Portland State University
Portland, Oregon
    Former Pastor
    Mount Zion Lutheran Church
    Detroit, Michigan

Dr. Warren A. Sorteberg
Director for Urban Ministry, Evangelism, and Advocacy
Division for Outreach
Evangelical Lutheran Church in America
Chicago, Illinois

Dr. Wayne Stumme, Director
Institute for Mission in the U.S.A.
Trinity Lutheran Seminary
Columbus, Ohio

The Rev. James R. Thomas
Assistant to the Bishop for Urban Ministry
Minneapolis Area Synod
Evangelical Lutheran Church in America
    Former Pastor
    The Lutheran Church of the Advent
    New York City

Dr. Margaret Wold
Religion Department
California Lutheran University
Thousand Oaks, California
    Former Community Resources Associate
    Division for Service and Mission in America
    The American Lutheran Church

Editor's Preface

This is the second book compiled by the Institute for Mission in the U.S.A. on the subject of mission and ministry. *The Experience of Hope* describes Lutheran efforts to carry out the church's mission and to exercise its ministry in the changing urban communities of the United States.

Our sincere thanks go to the parish pastors and the mission executives who contributed to this effort. We are grateful to the Rev. Nancy Koester for her careful editing of the manuscript and to the editorial staff at Augsburg Fortress for their patient cooperation. The major costs involved in the preparation of this book were covered by a generous grant from Aid Association for Lutherans, a fraternal benefit society with offices in Appleton, Wisconsin.

The Institute for Mission in the U.S.A. is an agency of partnership in mission within the Evangelical Lutheran Church in America. Its program emphases include evangelization, crosscultural mission and ministry, mission and ministry with the poor, and theological reflection on issues of mission. Offices of the Institute are located at Trinity Lutheran Seminary, Columbus, Ohio.

Introduction

Wayne Stumme

Therefore, since we are justified by faith, we have peace with God through our Lord Jesus Christ, through whom we have obtained access to this grace in which we stand; and we boast in our hope of sharing the glory of God. And not only that, but we also boast in our sufferings, knowing that suffering produces endurance, and endurance produces character, and character produces hope, and hope does not disappoint us, because God's love has been poured into our hearts through the Holy Spirit that has been given to us.

Romans 5:1-5

Part One

"And hope does not disappoint us." There is no more fitting way to begin a book about the church's mission and ministry in changing urban communities than by recalling St. Paul's stirring summary of the meaning of hope for the life and service of Christians. Writing to believers in the chief city of the Roman Empire, the apostle's words bring to a climax the argument he is making in this great epistle. They speak with equal force to us today.

Because God has chosen to justify sinners through Jesus Christ, Paul declares, a new and hopeful horizon has been opened for all humanity. Even now, the experience of peace with God, actualized in the loving relationship accomplished by the Spirit, directs us to the final unfolding of hope in the unbroken communion of life in the coming kingdom of God. And even now that hope is active, for it guides our choices and strengthens us in our struggles and renews us for the tasks which await us day by day.

9

This book, therefore, describes the efforts and convictions of persons inspired by that hope. The church is commissioned to bring the message of that hope to the inhabitants of our cities. Before all else, that message offers to all persons the promise of life which originates and continues through the gracious working of God in Jesus Christ. The authors of this volume are convinced that the men, women, and children of our urban communities need the consolation and the challenge of that gospel. They are equally certain that the uniquely compelling message of God's good work in Christ both reaches the inner lives of urban dwellers and addresses the circumstances of their social existence as well.

Thus, in speaking about that hope and its meaning for the city, this book must also take up those issues of suffering, endurance, and character—as Paul reminds us—that in their own way attest the present reality of the gracious promise. There can be no doubt that they, too, are part of the experience of ministry in our urban centers. The following pages will recount the struggles, failures, and successes of parish pastors and mission executives who have sought to advance the ministry of the church in the cities of America. As they would be the first to acknowledge, their persistence, resourcefulness, and vision have been nourished by the grace they have proclaimed and by which they have lived.

Part Two

Why was this book written? What do the authors intend to accomplish? It represents, first, an attempt to review Lutheran attitudes and practice in response to the emergence of an increasingly urbanized American society. Summaries of mission efforts by the former Lutheran Church in America and the former American Lutheran Church depict the beginnings of this involvement. These churches have now come together in the new Evangelical Lutheran Church in America, and this book brings together much of what they have learned and seeks to pass it on to this generation of those entrusted with the church's mission in the city. There is an honest recounting of failures as well as of our modest successes. Most importantly, this book describes what Lutherans still have to learn if they are to render faithful and effective service in the name of Christ within this country's urban communities.

Second, this book offers firsthand reports by pastors who have served in urban ministry. Most of them speak of their work among persons of color, persons of varied cultural and linguistic heritages, and persons who endure severe economic deprivation. A more comprehensive account of urban ministry, of course, would include descriptions of ministry in European ethnic communities, middle-class and upper-class neighborhoods, and the suburbs. The focus of this book is different: most of the ministries presented here have grown out of traditional Lutheran congregations located in what are now ethnically transitional neighborhoods. While the narratives of these ministries reflect the frustration and discouragement these pastors frequently endure, they also celebrate the encouraging—if fragile—signs of new life within situations often abandoned by others to decay and death.

Finally, the purpose of this book is to do more than learn from the past and acknowledge the insights of contemporary urban ministry; it is to express the church's continuing commitment to mission in the urban centers of this nation. One author, for example, reflects upon what has been done (and left undone) in order to advance new possibilities for ministry in the city. A mission executive suggests the directions the church's mission in the city will follow in the years ahead. Lessons from the global phenomenon of urbanization and from the efforts of other churches are summarized in a concluding essay.

In brief, this book constitutes a benchmark for American Lutherans committed to mission and ministry in urban centers of this country. It is not a comprehensive picture of all that Lutherans have done and are doing in American cities. The shortcomings of Lutheran strategy and practice are not obscured; the failures of understanding and vision are clearly noted. This volume, however, is far more than a lament and it is not an admission of defeat. As never before, the Lutheran church in the United States is acknowledging urban ministry as the great mission challenge of our time. These pages are intended as a positive contribution to the church's assumption of its mission tasks in the growing and changing cities of our society.

Part Three

Having come this far, what have we learned? The authors of this volume have made significant contributions to our understanding of urban mission and ministry. The experiences and insights of other Christians in this country and elsewhere have provided valuable correctives and have stimulated new approaches to ministry in the city. Social scientists have helped us grasp the complexities of urban existence, and have compelled us to recognize the cultural diversity which confronts us in metropolitan areas. And we continue to be instructed by those men and women who embody the Christian hope in parish ministries and secular callings, and whose faithfulness directs us to dimensions of the church's mission which dare not be ignored. The following, at the very least, we have learned.

Theological integrity. The urban context of Christian mission is characterized both by religious diversity and by secular indifference. What, then, is the unique and indispensable message of the church as it ministers to those who live in the modern city? How can the gospel be proclaimed in ways that are both relevant and faithful? How can we know what we may affirm within this bewildering cultural milieu, and what we must reject? Critically and sensitively appropriated, the insights of the Lutheran confessional tradition continue to demonstrate their usefulness. A mission theology for urban ministry must maintain biblical fidelity in confessing the christological and trinitarian dimensions of the Christian faith in its contemporary engagement with society and culture. That essential identity cannot be compromised.

Cultural sensitivity. The gracious word we have been given to speak is meant to be heard by persons representing the full spectrum of religious, ethnic, class, and linguistic differences. In their encounter with Lutheran congregations, they respond with a willingness to share their own traditions, experiences, and insights. Many of these seem to challenge accepted patterns in Lutheran churches. Liturgical forms, educational methods, leadership styles, and stewardship practices frequently are questioned by newcomers who want to contribute something of their past to the congregations they have joined. Although this development may cause tension within the Christian community, it basically must be viewed as a positive occurrence. The question faced by many urban congregations is simply this: what will guide us as we preserve the best of our heritage and, at the same time, appropriate the new gifts that others bring to our common life? This issue calls for the cooperative efforts of pastors and lay leaders, liturgical scholars, musicians, sociologists, and theologians.

Social critique and action. Every city is a complex of social institutions, attitudes, and practices. Lutheran practitioners of urban ministry have demonstrated only limited understanding of these social realities. Our customary focus on individuals and their pastoral care has not prepared us for the responsibility of working with— and, sometimes, against—those political and economic entities that decisively shape urban life. Most pastors lack the critical tools that would enable them to recognize the self-interest and exploitation of persons which frequently mark the activities of these institutions. We have yet to explore the full possibilities of cooperation with community organizations and union locals in dealing with community problems. The victimization of those neighborhoods in which our congregations are located continues unchecked. The time has come to recognize that the hope that the gospel engenders cannot be limited to the consolation of individuals; its social consequences must be recognized, and acted upon. This, too, belongs to the future of urban mission and ministry.

Ministry to all of life. The stories narrated by urban pastors in this book express their common conviction that the church's ministry in the city must embrace life in its totality. Central to all that the church does is that essential service in which the grace of Christ is proclaimed to women, men, and children and through which sacramental incorporation and nurture become actual for them. The brutalities of much urban existence, however, compel us to confront those attitudes and practices and social structures that threaten to diminish life and to deny the dignity God has given to all. The city's children and young people must have major claim upon our efforts and resources; they in particular are victims of deprivation of all kinds; and they have a biblical right to the compassion pastors and congregations must demonstrate. We cannot forget, of course, those many others who are at risk: single parents, young and poorly educated men and women, the unemployed and the underemployed, the recently incarcerated, those struggling with various addictions, the mentally ill, the aging, and the homeless. As congregations respond to these situations of desperate need, they will innovate in ways unknown to previous generations of Christians. This volume provides examples of some of these promising initiatives.

Preparing leadership for urban ministry. Few pastors or lay leaders in urban ministries believe the church prepared them adequately for this work. If, as many contend, urban ministry is the critical frontier of mission for the church in our time, then the seminaries of the church have an urgent responsibility to reexamine curricula and teaching methods and extra-seminary education. This effort will require the closest cooperation among urban pastors, seminary faculty, and mission executives if the Lutheran church is to prepare men and women for the demands and possibilities inherent in urban mission today.

"And hope does not disappoint us." Our best insights and our most strenuous efforts find their meaning only within the context of God's gracious turning to humanity in his Son, Jesus Christ. That is "the grace in which we stand," and that is the grace we would make known in the urban communities of this nation.

PART ONE

Impelled by Hope:
the Beginnings of Lutheran Mission
in Changing Urban Communities

CHAPTER **1**

The History of the Lutheran Church in Urban Mission

Robert S. Hoyt

For many years the Lutheran church identified the people of Germany and Scandinavia as its primary mission responsibility. When these Lutherans arrived in North America, the Lutheran church followed the immigrant stream through the urban centers of the East Coast to the agricultural plains of the Midwest. It seemed natural for denominational leaders to pursue a concept of ministry among "our people."

After World War II this country experienced a major change in urban settlement. Suburbs enveloped central cities. An unprecedented baby boom altered family life, and large-scale relocation to the suburbs resulted. The church followed Lutherans to these places and viewed this as the appropriate service of "our people." The movement of Lutherans to California, Texas, and Florida resulted in major mission expansion in the Sunbelt. At one time, for example, the American Lutheran Church had one-third of its Church Extension Fund (its mortgage loan money) invested in the state of California.

Suburban growth along arterial highways provided numerous locations for new church development. Many new congregations were formed during this period of rapid expansion between 1950 and 1968. A package mission program provided church property and called a pastor even before any new members for the congregation had been gathered. While generally successful during this era, this single-strategy approach did not apply to diverse American communities. During the 1960s, church leaders began to recognize that many mission starts were not functioning according to the model. This first strategy of new church development typically had staff who were committed to service to Lutheran constituencies and to sound economic return. During this period, the church slowly recognized two things: first, new congregations were starting to receive members from non-Lutheran traditions (Protestant, Catholic, or Jewish) or who were unchurched. Even though the mission policy was directed toward Lutherans, these congregations were serving a more diverse population than the previous German or Scandinavian traditions. Second, in the 1960s the church began to experience dying congregations in both rural and inner-city areas. While new congregations were being formed in suburban areas, an almost equal number of congregations were going out of existence. When a congregation was closed, one-third transferred to another Lutheran congregation, one-third joined another Christian congregation, and the remaining third seemed to drop out of active membership in any congregation.

Our urban consciousness, influenced by the civil rights movement and the riots of the late 1960s, was growing during this period. As an expression of this awareness, a new strategy for urban ministry was inaugurated. As neighborhoods changed from white ethnic to pluralistic, black, or other nonwhite communities, an urban church strategy of *withdrawal* or *preservation* was followed. This was the first of several urban strategies, and it came too late and offered too little. Either intentionally or by default, church leaders identified those city congregations that could continue in their ministry and those that could not. Those in the second category were closed, relocated to suburban areas, or subsidized because their presence in that location, or a continued ministry to that constituency, was important to the church.

In most cases, these strategies of withdrawal or preservation considered only what was happening to the members of the congregation. If the members moved away, the congregation followed. A declining congregation's neighborhood often was populated by more people than had lived there before, even though their ethnic origin differed from that of the original community. Church leaders would sell church property and participate in the final worship on a Sunday morning with the small remnant of the old congregation.

17

Later that same day, they would turn the deed over to a new congregation of a different denomination. Actively reaching out to the people of the neighborhood, the new congregation would hold worship with over 300 persons in attendance. This Lutheran strategy depended heavily upon statistical analysis; for instance, multiracial communities required 30,000–45,000 people to justify a continued Lutheran presence, while a white area only needed a potential of 5,000–15,000 persons to justify the establishment of a new congregation. The disproportionate share of mission dollars invested in such ministry starts versus those designated for urban ministry, and the increased awareness of the urban crisis during the 1960s, gave birth to the Conference on Inner-City Ministry (CICM). In 1968, CICM's anger forced the church to increase support to congregations dedicated to staying in the city. A crisis fund, later known as the Development Assistant Program, was also established. Those urban pastors also worked for a change in Lutheran mission leadership.

The second urban strategy was *coexistence* within changing neighborhoods. The leaders of the church's American mission effort represented this strategy. These pastors, who had opened their buildings to the community, assumed that if persons in the community used the church building, they would become involved in the congregation. There was no real attempt, however, to change the power structure of the congregation, and the new people who joined remained outsiders. They were not part of the traditional Lutheran ethnic identities, and frequently found that the Lutheran liturgy and music did not take into account their own spiritual journeys. This era lasted only five to six years. By 1974 the American Lutheran Church restructured and had created the Division for Service and Mission in America. A new strategy called *adaptation* was developed. This strategy went beyond coexistence by helping the existing ministry reach out to the residents of a community. The congregation pledged that the needs of current members would be served while at the same time additional staff would reach out to the new population of the community. Often these congregations added non-whites and persons whose primary language was other than English to the congregational staff. These new staff persons generated programs designed to meet community needs, often creating social ministry projects such as food banks, health clinics, and tutoring programs. The congregation could also join with other churches and community groups to develop new community organizations. These organizations were frequently controversial and sometimes confrontational. They placed increasing emphasis on housing development and the creation of opportunities for employment. This approach sought to transform the community by bringing in new resources and improving the quality of life of its residents. Often the members of the congregation were not involved in these strategies. The professional program staff they had added carried out these programs apart from the daily life of the congregation.

During this time church leaders were influenced by university urban affairs departments, which were exploring systems theories of urban dynamics. The church engaged in a process of urban planning and demographic studies, which led to a series of *cooperative ministries*. This strategy gave birth to Lutheran councils in cities like Baltimore, Washington, Denver, and Kansas City. It attempted to design specialized ministries in order to serve the unreached people in society. In Minneapolis for instance, Lutherans developed a singles ministry, and in Chicago they provided a ministry for the entertainment of night people in the city. These "shepherd of the streets" ministries relied upon intercongregational cooperation to meet the unique needs of special groups.

A number of denominations began to work together to establish support services to aid in the development of urban ministry. Cooperative programs at the national level such as the Urban Training Center, the National Parish Training Lab, and the Joint Strategy and Action Committee were examples of denominational cooperation. For the most part these were efforts of the church bureaucracy, and they had a minimal effect on congregations carrying out ministry in urban communities.

An additional strategy developed during this era of cooperation led to specialization of ministries among blacks, Hispanics, Asians, and American Indians. Increased financial support to these ethnic ministries took some money away from traditional new congregational starts. This shift was justified because cities, which had once expanded along the expressways, were now filling in the spaces between expressways with new housing developments. Churches started in the late sixties and early seventies could now serve these rapidly expanding communities. The church's mission dollars were available for this outreach, which included persons of color or language other than English. While new congregational starts dropped to a low of twelve starts per year during the mid-1970s, these outreach ministries began to diversify the constituency of the former American Lutheran Church. The major emphasis during this era, however, was not on persons of color or language other than English but on experimentation in ministry. One congregation might deal with the issue of ecology and another with ministry for retarded children, while still others were experimenting with house-church or special issue congregations.

Few of these alternative forms of ministry ever became viable congregations. We began to learn that participation in God's mission meant taking mission seriously. Lessons of effective ministry learned during the church's suburban expansion have helped to focus our efforts on the *rerooting of ministry in the urban place*. This means that the congregation seeks to be in ministry with the people where it is located. The identification of and development of indigenous leadership as the primary leadership of the congregation is still a major task as this new urban strategy based on the rerooting of the congregation in the neighborhood takes shape. While this leadership development is a key issue, the rerooting of urban ministry directs us to other concerns which will require the church's attention in the next decade.

The empowerment of the poor.   The church will need to learn to work with the poor so that their lives may be lived above despair, their human dignity be affirmed, and their fuller participation in the benefits and obligations of American society be encouraged.

Racial and economic inclusiveness.   The church will need to foster the genuine interdependence of people of different ethnic and socioeconomic groups in order that the oneness of God's people may be acknowledged in the sharing of their gifts and insights.

Development of concepts of the family.   The church must find ways to nurture families. The church will need to empower and equip people to care for children in ways that contribute to their

20

growth as healthy, sensitive, and responsible members of American society.

The centralization of economic power.   The manipulation and disruption of communities through the closing of plants and production centers is a growing concern for urban congregational life. The shifting focus of the U.S. economy toward service occupations and transnational production calls the church to commit itself to develop economic stability and fairness within society.

Families headed by females.   Households where single women head families require attention, especially where poverty exists, and women and children suffer from violence.

Congregational interdependence.   For too long autonomy has been taken for granted in church life. An interdependent approach links each congregation into the mission and ministry of other congregations.

Renewal of urban church property.   Many urban church properties are old and decaying; others were built without wheelchair or other special-needs access. The rebuilding of this property so that it will be accessible and efficient will be costly, but it needs to be done.

Development of responsive liturgy.   The church intends to reach out to persons whose cultures differ from those found in traditional Lutheranism. Meaningful worship will require that liturgies and music reflect the different Christian heritages of the people in the place where the congregation serves.

Commitment to social justice.   A recovery of Christian commitment to social justice will require the church to reform its identity and perhaps risk the loss of popular support. Religious privatization may be a threat to the integrity of the gospel.

Development of mission partnership.   Cooperation between congregations must cut across the lines of class, race, and culture.

Such interdependence is essential for the growth and development of Christian mission in America. The church serves a rapidly changing environment and strives to find appropriate strategies for mission. In response to these challenges, it has developed area strategies and new coalitions to assist in the development of urban congregational life. Yet the congregation is still basic for carrying out mission in America. The strengthening of the congregation as it responds to the needs of its people and community is essential to accomplishing that mission.

CHAPTER **2**

The Lutheran Church and Urban Ministry in North America: An Overview

Harvey S. Peters, Jr.

This chapter surveys the attempts by Lutheran churches in the United States to do ministry in cities.

Historical Background

After World War II, the Lutheran churches were largely comprised of the descendants of immigrants from northern and eastern Europe. In the late 1940s and 1950s, the Lutheran church assisted thousands of immigrants to this country. Many congregations, especially those with eastern European roots, grew because of the newly arrived families from "the other side." Many, if not most, of these Lutheran congregations were located in large cities. At this time, over two-thirds of all Lutherans lived in cities, not unlike the general population. Lutherans maintained a strong loyalty to their churches in the various ethnic and cultural traditions. Most of the growth in these congregations came from birth and baptism within the membership or through immigration.

During the forties and fifties, evangelism or outreach sought to recapture disenchanted Lutherans or maintain ties with Lutherans who had moved. As late as 1958, it was still the policy of American mission boards to establish "new missions" where surveys showed sufficient numbers of Lutherans to support new congregations.

In the meantime, the nation was in the midst of major changes that would affect the cities and the Lutheran church dramatically. Urbanologists still debate about what primary forces shaped the cities of the U.S. after World War II. At least two major changes affected the ministry of the Lutheran church: (1) the increasing minority populations moving to the cities, and (2) the growth of the suburbs. Perhaps the former hastened the latter.

Returning from the military were large numbers of persons of color who had served side by side with whites. With the expansion of a postwar economy, many of these veterans sought jobs in the city. The U.S. government provided low-interest loans which enabled veterans to buy housing. The housing market, however, was segregated by race. The personal prejudices of the majority were being institutionalized, and the combined practices of the real estate industry, insurance companies, and banks maintained segregated housing patterns.

At the same time the U.S. government provided large sums of money to local and state transportation authorities to build a network of highway systems. These highways provided easy access to inexpensive land surrounding the cities. Housing developments and subdivisions started to spring up around almost every major city. For many whites, this was an opportunity to develop a new way of life for themselves and their children. But persons of color found the suburbs difficult if not impossible to enter.

In many city neighborhoods, blockbusting was in full swing. This practice expressed both racial prejudice and fear of economic loss. A real estate agent would approach a homeowner in a white neighborhood and suggest that a "colored" family had purchased a home nearby. The agent would suggest that a rash of sales to other blacks, Hispanics, or other minorities was about to begin. Then the agent would offer to buy the house at a stated price—usually below market value. Because it was difficult for persons of color to buy decent housing, the agent would sell the newly acquired house to them at a "bargain price"—usually well above the market value. This spurred "the white flight" to the suburbs.

The shifting population generated changes in public institutions. Political and economic power shifted to the suburbs. City schools, health-care facilities, services, commerce, and the urban intrastructure declined. The cities were increasingly places for the very poor or the very rich. The suburbs became the home of the white middle class, of persons more highly educated, more affluent, and more isolated from the city.

These inequities and injustices did not continue unchallenged. During the 1960s the nation was faced with its most severe internal crisis since the Civil War. Black people rebelled. From Birmingham, Alabama, to Boston, Massachusetts, from Watts in Los Angeles to Washington, D.C., one city after another erupted. These rebellions—called race riots by the majority population—awakened the nation to the long years of injustices. Meanwhile the involvement of the U.S. in an unpopular war in Vietnam, a war fought against people of color, awakened in other people of color a sense of "kinship" with people who were oppressed by the white "super powers." The issue of racism took on global dimensions, especially in those cities of North America where the largest concentration of persons of color lived.

The Lutheran church, like other mainline denominations, responded to these new realities in a variety of ways. Just as some practices in society had been modified over the past two decades, the stance of the Lutheran church in urban ministry also evolved. The Lutheran churches reviewed their policies and practices. Theological and biblical study resulted in many courageous and controversial social statements intended to educate the membership on subjects such as economic justice, race relations, world community, and civil disobedience. Churchwide priority programs for social justice were adopted and major fund appeals were developed to support ministries that would address social change—especially in the cities.

Urban ministry as we now know it, developed in various stages, which are outlined below.

Strategies of Withdrawal and Preservation

Relocate. Like other churches, the Lutherans moved to the suburbs. A study developed by the University of Michigan showed that over thirty Lutheran congregations moved to the suburbs of Detroit between 1955 and 1965. Usually the new building was built near the new residences of members who had moved out of the city. In many cases, especially during the 1950s, these moves were assisted by policies of the judicatories (Synods/Districts) and church-wide mission boards.

Merge or yoke with another Lutheran congregation. Some congregations tried to survive by sharing a pastor or consolidating their congregations. This usually resulted in a shrinking membership and program.

Close. This was the ultimate withdrawal strategy. In some cases the remaining assets and/or building were turned over to the judicatories for use or sale.

None of these strategies attempted to shape the ministry of the congregation to its location. The congregation was thought to exist for its members alone.

Strategies of Coexistence with the Changing Neighborhood

Opening facilities for the use of community groups. To be a good neighbor, the congregation let groups like Alcoholics Anonymous, Boy and Girl Scouts, school programs, and similar social groups rent space in their facilities.

Welcoming neighbors to activities of the church. The congregation's sign indicated that "all are welcome." Members still living in the neighborhood were encouraged to let neighbors know they were welcome.

In these strategies, the congregations did not change their programs but sought to make them available to others. The congregation existed to serve its members, but others were welcome. Unless the congregation had an endowment or a loyal group that supported it, these strategies did not suffice. In some cases, congregations voted to "remain in the neighborhood." Pastors and members living elsewhere, who returned to the neighborhood on Sunday, often created a credibility problem in the neighborhood.

Strategies of Adaptation

Adding staff. If the exclusive responsibility of the existing staff was to serve the membership of the congregation, other staff members, such as youth workers, community pastors or lay associates, could be added. In some cases these new staff persons were of the predominant racial or ethnic group in the neighborhood. These staff persons were to serve as a bridge between the members and the community.

Adding programs to meet the needs of the community. These varied programs were usually designed to meet some social ministry need. Such programs included health clinics, tutoring students, athletic clubs, homemaking classes, fellowship activities, food pantries, and outlets for clothing and household appliances.

Community organizing. Efforts to organize the people in neighborhoods for self-determination were a major emphasis during the late 1960s and remains so to some degree today. Organizations guided by Industrial Areas Foundations, founded by Saul Alinsky, were among the best efforts toward this end. Many pastors received training to organize and assist such local groups. The most lasting benefits came when these organizations moved from purely confrontational political issues to economic development activities, resulting in housing and jobs.

Many congregations began to recognize that they had to be more than simply "open" to the community. In most cases the resources with which to reach out were not sufficient, so congregations applied for funds from their judicatories or mission boards. During the 1960s, the denominations first started to develop churchwide funds and staff for urban concerns and community organizing.

The result was various valuable ministries. Persons were served in many ways. In retrospect, however, many people were treated like clients rather than members of the family of faith. Some of their needs were met, but their personal involvement was seldom sought. Many congregations were very active and busy, but not really changed by the realities of the city or neighborhood in which they were called to do ministry. The illusion was one of involvement because of "serving" the neighborhood. In too many cases the neighborhood was being kept at an arm's length with the "add-on" programs serving as a barrier rather than a bridge to full involvement with the community.

Strategies of Cooperation

Inter-Lutheran planning. The National Lutheran Council (NLC) was the most notable Lutheran effort at cooperating in urban ministry during the 1960s. Following that, the Lutheran Council in the United States became a program agency for many cooperative endeavors. The urban studies of the NLC made churches more aware of the need for greater cooperation at the local level. Early attempts were made to get urban and suburban congregations to cooperate.

Formation of citywide cooperative ministries. Across the country, congregations of the Lutheran churches were organizing cooperative ministries with the approval and financial support of the judicatories and churchwide offices. These cooperatives normally dealt with noncongregational ministries. The general principle for organizing the cooperative ministry was either, "We will do together what none of us can do alone," or "As Lutherans we need to build strength upon strength to have a voice in changing the society."

Shepherds of the street. In several cities, such as Cleveland and the twin cities of Minneapolis and St. Paul, pastors were called by the judicatories and funded by churchwide offices to do ministry with people on the "fringe" of society. They became counselors, friends, brokers, and advocates for people who could not fit into the systems of society.

Denominational developments. Other denominations were facing the same problems in attempting to relate to the realities of urbanization. The Lutheran churches joined with others in the formation of the Joint Action and Strategy Committee in order to coordinate their resources nationally and regionally. The Lutherans participated in the Chicago-based "Urban Institute for Christian Mission" which served as a training ground for church leaders. Participants lived for three days on the streets of Chicago without money or identification in a "plunge" to see what it was like to cope under such circumstances. All bishops of the Lutheran Church in America participated in this during the late 1960s.

At this stage of development, the consciousness of the church was raised regarding urban ministries. The major studies in several cities sometimes resulted in cooperative ministries being formed. Some outstanding ones remain today. Their programs tended to be social ministry such as low-income housing, services to the aging, youth ministry, and liaison work with people not being served adequately by the congregations.

While the ministry of the Lutheran churches in the cities grew through these efforts, the basic composition of the existing church was not significantly changed. These strategies usually had a non-congregational emphasis for urban ministry. The positive part of this was the urging of the whole church to become aware of its responsibility for all peoples in the cities. The negative part was that these strategies did not face the fact that the Lutheran church in the cities was shrinking. The assumption that studies, consciousness raising, and cooperation with others would "trickle down" to the congregations was largely mistaken—even when reinforced by financial assistance from judicatories and churchwide agencies.

Strategies of Specialized and Experimental Ministries

Establishment of separate ministries for people of color and primary language other than English.   Frustrated in attempts to survive in the cities, the Lutheran churches tried to develop a critical mass of minority members within its fellowship. In some cases, minority pastors from other denominations were sought to become Lutheran pastors and start congregations among their own racial or ethnic groups. Some came into the Lutheran church with a congregation from their former denomination.

Developing alternate forms of congregational life. The Lutheran churches tried many experimental ministries, including the use of "store-front" buildings, "tentmaker" ministries, housing projects managed by pastors, and the use of mass media to attract persons to the Lutheran church.

Valuable information was gained through these strategies, but often with little result for the larger church. "Alternative" congregations or "black ministries" or "Hispanic ministries" were often isolated from one another.

Networks such as the Conference of Inner City Ministries of the former American Lutheran Church were created to break down this isolation. Meanwhile caucuses or conferences comprised of people of particular racial or ethnic groups have developed, and each in its own way has helped urban ministry in the Lutheran church.

Strategies of Replanting and Redeveloping the Church in the Cities

Neighborhood ministry. During the 1960s several congregations began rerooting themselves in their neighborhoods seeking to identify fully with the neighborhood in which they were called. Pastors and their families moved into the neighborhood in which they would do ministry. Respect for the church grew as the symbols, music, and culture of the neighborhood people enhanced the worship. The racial, economic, and social makeup of the neighborhood was increasingly reflected in the membership, worship, and leadership of the congregation. The church became a part of the neighborhood. No longer was the Word and Sacrament ministry separated from service or social change. The pastor and congregation became the Lutheran church for that place.

Inclusive ministry. Since most cities are comprised of diverse people, the Lutheran church tried to include people of color and primary language other than English in its membership. Not satisfied to start new ministries among minority groups alone, or to develop ministries that were racially or economically homogeneous, the Lutheran church sought diversity. At this time, the minority membership of the Lutheran church bodies is less than 2 percent of the total membership. The minority membership is growing approximately one-third faster than white membership. It will be a long time before the Lutheran church reflects the same ratio as that of the United States, which is closer to 20 percent. Most of the racial and economic diversity within the Lutheran church is nevertheless a direct result of ministries in the cities.

Interdependence, mutual support, and accountability. Since 1964 and the formation of the Center City Lutheran Parish in Philadelphia, the Lutheran church has built coalitions in the cities. The purpose of these coalitions is to support Lutheran congregations as they reroot themselves in their neighborhoods. In contrast to cooperative ministries, coalitions concern themselves with all dimensions of the ministry, including evangelism, congregational development, and social justice. Pastors serving congregations in these coalitions are accountable to each other in carrying out neighborhood ministry. Each coalition has a director who is a teacher and leader. These coalition directors are linked to one another through the offices of the churchwide agencies.

Urban ministry as ministry to the whole church. The bishop plays an important role through careful intervention, support, and recommendation of appropriate pastors who can break patterns of exclusiveness and redevelop congregations that serve their neighborhoods. The policies of the whole church have been shaped through a careful, sometimes difficult, but usually deliberate exchange among all parts of the church engaged in urban ministry. Through this process urban ministry has moved from the fringe to a central position in the priorities of the church.

Policies regarding the use of financial support to congregations, the training of pastors, the placement of seminary interns, repair and renovation of church buildings, and the use of World Hunger Funds for advocacy of justice have all been informed by urban ministry. The emphasis on the rediscovery of the "parish as place" learned through this experience is influencing ministry development in various settings.

Summary

The Lutheran church has come to its present stance with great struggle. As we have become more rooted in the cities and more fully engaged in the hopes and struggles of the people of the cities, we have been changed. Where change has occurred, there is much to be thankful for and much to celebrate. But the sins of racism, sexism, and classism are still powerful forces in our church and cities. The gospel of Jesus Christ compels the church to proclaim the kingdom that has come and is yet coming. The pain and promise of that struggle is real, because North American cities are the Third World in microcosm. For that reason, we have much to share with and learn from our sister churches doing ministry in other parts of the world.

PART TWO

Sustained by Hope:
the Present Experience of Ministry
in Changing Urban Communities

CHAPTER **3**

Dynamics of Theology and Practice in Urban Ministry

Harold D. Schlactenhaufen

The city is constantly changing. It is beset with the evils of chronic unemployment, poverty, racism, classism, violence, and the systemic misuse of people. The destruction and exploitation in the city and the cultural development and religious expression that seek to save the city are always in conflict. This "war" can be understood as the conflict between darkness and light, flesh and spirit, falsehood and truth, principalities and the kingdom of Christ. This means that our theology and practice, while rooted in Scripture and Christian tradition, are challenged to grow with the changing urban scene. No one style of ministry or theology, therefore, can provide a final definition of urban ministry now or in the future.

The inner city is a dumping ground for people released from institutions or consigned to halfway houses, and those left adrift by family, friends, or neighbors. The city clearly shows that there are gaping holes in the "safety net" described by a former president and that for some this net never existed. Neglected people will congregate at any church or agency that extends even a modicum of compassion. Lazarus stands at the door. We cannot ignore such people and still be servants of Christ. Ministry in the inner city is called to respond to society's greatest concentration of social fallout.

There is a distinct milieu in some inner-city neighborhoods that has never existed before. One has to experience this in order to identify it. It includes a sense of the permanency (not hopelessness) of a large underclass. There is little opportunity for individual development. In part, explicit racism has given way to explicit classism (undergirded by an implicit racism). Social and business institutions increasingly rely on "disinformation" or lying. General disrespect for others and indifference to personal or communal responsibility affects a large number of young males (primarily black) who are unemployed and left adrift. These forces in the low-income areas of the city have created a unique set of priorities. This is not to say that all or even most people show negative characteristics. On the contrary, the people of the inner city are for the most part remarkable folk who show unusual strength of character, patience, inner beauty, and a forthrightness that emerges from perseverance. It is difficult for outsiders to understand this.

No wonder, then, that many assumptions about and expectations of urban ministry (held by people living outside of the inner city) are misleading, if not false. Consider, for example, how the church subsidizes (or provides mission support and partners for) congregations whose members are too poor to maintain a minimal ministry. Pastors and members of those congregations consistently report that they are restricted in ministry, treated with disrespect, and asked to dispose of all liquid assets before receiving any financial assistance. Then they are required to submit monthly financial accounting forms to qualify for the next month's payment. We already have many checks and balances on our ministry through the office of the bishop, and these additional restrictive and condescending policies are unnecessary. Those in urban ministry clearly have a different understanding of financial support than those who have the responsibility of dispensing this aid.

Meanwhile, those in urban ministry must cope with unique pressures. Population density, for example, is both a blessing and a curse. More people means greater potential for services, benefits, friendships, ideas, and diversity. But it also means increased exploitation, irritation, disruption, and the violence endemic to poverty and chronic unemployment. If one moves into the inner city, all insurance premiums (except life insurance) will double in cost. The need for personal security increases markedly. Accessibility to low-cost shopping is limited. People in the congregation and community

35

have greater need for pastoral assistance, and this means more referrals, more counseling, and more requests for help in securing food, shelter, clothing, housing, jobs, and education. Existing social service agencies and public programs are insufficient and often impersonal. Inner-city congregations are often low on resources, forced to pay low salaries to clergy, and frequently are insufficiently supported by the rest of the church. Increased demand combined with decreased resources creates a situation of frustration and broken promises. The church could help most by providing additional subsidized clergy staff to work in these congregations and more resources (including funds) to develop mission programs in the inner city.

Many areas of the inner city are "foreign mission fields" because they contain a variety of cultures. For instance, there is not a single "black experience" or "Hispanic style," any more than there is only one "white type." The city is a place of radically different life-styles including trends and fads, and also reflecting changing values, attitudes, and beliefs.

Subcultures within the city often develop an "in-house" language. Slang, the creation of new words, alternative grammar and syntax represent a worldview that is foreign to a church publishing house, a middle-class executive, or a traditional academic discipline. There is no dictionary for this urban language but rather a world of perceptions and experiences. This means that "missionaries" have to be sent into this "foreign country" for long periods of time to learn the language.

Since the erosion of one dominant Western worldview in the twentieth century, many worldviews—all claiming to be the most reasonable or truthful—have emerged. In the core city, people representing different backgrounds, experiences, classes, nations, and races rub shoulders with one another in commerce, employment, cultural arts, religion, government, and education. The cross-fertilization of their approaches and beliefs has produced a super-market of options in which people select worldviews in every combination imaginable. People do not fit into customary categories, and many hold views considered by some to be inconsistent with the gospel. The church must take care not to alienate people who hold these "foreign" worldviews. Inner-city ministry, in particular, must break free from the practice of repeating theological formulas (whether in adult instruction, worship, or evangelism) that make no attempt to open up communication with these persons. The inner city, like a foreign mission field, is polytheistic. This means that for many, including Christians, the "one Lord" is of merely equal importance with other lords. For many non-Christians, this includes belief in godlike powers ruling their lives.

The issue for the Christian is not whether one believes in God, but rather in which god one believes. Whatever is most important to a person is their god, as Luther made clear in his explanation of the first commandment. In earlier forms of polytheism there were gods for different needs, desires, situations, and fears. Today these gods include self, the nation, our economic system, forms of recreation, other persons, jobs, and dependencies (drugs, sex, etc.). These gods reward and punish, promote and demote, eliminate, and claim to save. They take many forms and shapes; they can also be institutionalized and systemic. Their existence is based on a belief system that rewards selfishness. There are many deeply Christian people in the inner city, but there is also an increasing number of people who have experienced the power of these competing gods. This is a serious matter for the proclamation and interpretation of the gospel.

Many people in the core city areas have heard the word Lutheran, but they have experienced Lutheran congregations as ethnic enclaves. They have seldom been exposed to Lutheran theology, particularly Lutheran theology that has been adapted to their situation.

Mt. Zion Evangelical Lutheran Church, Detroit, attempts to adapt Lutheran theology to the needs and experiences of diverse cultures in this city. In some ways the programs of Mt. Zion Evangelical Lutheran Church are much the same as one might find in any Evangelical Lutheran Church in America (ELCA) congregation. There are education, evangelism, stewardship, and worship. There are social concerns, property management, and personnel issues. The congregation also has various organizations for youth, women, men, couples, singles, seniors, acolytes, ushers, and study and prayer groups. But these programs must be carried out differently in the city.

In education, for example, the pastor must rewrite existing studies or create new material. Little published church material works in inner-city educational programming, in part because illiteracy and low reading ability are common among many residents of the core city. A significant number of people are bilingual or have a native language other than English. A pastor must be willing to learn another language and be open to hear the faith expressed in new ways.

For a number of reasons people from low-income families may not be attracted to educational programs. A pastor must initiate formal and informal educational programs which build on experiences and interests often different than the pastor's own.

At Mt. Zion, some English classes for refugees have expanded into a special program entitled "No Longer Strangers." This program, funded by the national church, offers instruction in Christian faith to Hmong people living near the church. This venture helps Hmong people to better understand the basic teachings of Christianity within American culture, and is well received by the Hmong community.

Evangelism at Mt. Zion includes a wide range of visitation and hospitality efforts such as greeters, coffee hours, and potlucks, church/community events, and personal identification techniques; sponsorship of new members; rides to church; newsletters, advertising, leaflets, brochures and bulletin boards; community surveys, door-to-door invitations, and the like. These activities are very time-consuming and leave little time for developing the deeper and more important meaning of evangelism.

What might "evangelism programs" mean in the inner city? First, depending on the size and type of facility the congregation owns, there is a great opportunity to provide meeting space (usually gratis) to community organizations. A step beyond this is to organize new groups that are needed for helping others (such as a neighborhood watch, adult literacy program, or public issue action groups). These efforts can be combined in a community center. Such community centers can provide additional programs for senior citizens, youth, children, mothers, and the unemployed. Organizing a full community center takes staff and volunteers, however, and inner-city congregations frequently lack resources for this, except as they add to their pastors' work loads.

Another possibility is to develop a cottage industry, housing corporation, urban renewal project, educational or treatment program such as halfway houses. At Mt. Zion, for example, we have developed both a community center and a cottage industry. The community center sponsors roller skating and recreation for youth, Boy Scouts, a summer youth program, after school tutoring for elementary grades, a women's exercise class, Alcoholics Anonymous, Narcotics Anonymous, Agoraphobics in Motion, English as a second language, sewing classes, offices for the Hmong community, an Emotional Recovery Group, Food and Friendship (for senior citizens), contracted services for senior citizens for Legal Aid, free health screening, flu shots, a food pantry, and clothes closet. The cottage industry supported by Mt. Zion is a Hmong Stitchery Cooperative. The co-op is now located in its own facility and is operating semi-independently. All of these programs, with few exceptions, are provided gratis by the congregation. They are an expensive, but vital expression of our mission in the inner city of Detroit. These community services and programs are as much an expression of evangelism as any other witness to our Christian faith. We do not establish community services to recruit members but to seek the good of our neighbors.

Stewardship at Mt. Zion includes people, ideas, organizations, symbols, and resources; it is attitudes and practices; it is what we do with ourselves and others. Inner-city congregations conduct year-around stewardship programs. One small part of stewardship might include fund-raising or the annual giving of offerings and tithes. But fund-raising appeals are not necessarily a part of Christian stewardship even if done in the name of Christ. The effectiveness of any appeal for funds is about the same in the inner city as anywhere else, the following considerations should be noted: first, lower-income folk give a higher percentage of their income than do the wealthy; second, it takes about 4.5 new giving units to replace one former giving unit in congregations moving from middle/upper class to low-income membership; third, low-income people usually are not accustomed or not able to tithe; and fourth, lack of funds to meet basic ministry needs is the most limiting factor in inner-city mission.

How can those engaged in urban ministry respond to these urgent financial needs? One way is to establish an endowment fund to underwrite the long-term commitment needed to build a multicultural congregation and to provide funds for alternative ministries working through local congregations.

Another approach is to apply to government programs or private foundations for program grants. The government, however, will not fund church activities because of the perceived need to maintain the separation of church and state; and foundations generally do not fund churches because of questions about their legal status as charitable organizations as well as the scope of their programs. The congregation can, however, form a subsidiary nonprofit corporation for community and neighborhood development. While this type of nonprofit corporation cannot engage in what the government classifies as "explicit religious activities," it can assist in nonlicensed educational, food, clothing, and housing programs.

Inner-city congregations with decreasing incomes and escalating expenses may also appeal to other congregations for help. Unfortunately, this is the most difficult. Although there are a few noncity congregations eager to help, most congregations typically respond negatively to appeals for financial assistance. There are many reasons for this, but there can be no question about the critical need for additional money for inner-city ministry. A final option is to allow the congregation to become weak through depletion of funds because the national, regional, or synodical church will give just enough money to keep the ministry breathing. In cases where such subsistence maintenance is provided, inner-city pastors may simply preside at the inevitable death of such congregations. Thus we bury viable and critical sites of mission and ministry. A better approach would be to institute long-range planning accompanied by the financial commitments necessary—not just to sustain but to develop inner-city ministries.

Worship in the inner-city congregation takes the liturgical and theological traditions of the church seriously as do all Lutheran congregations. Some adaptations, however, are made. Using a variety of settings enhances worship, and many congregations have added music that is not in the hymnal. We seek to bring our worship alive in new God-pleasing ways that enrich the whole body, finding consistent and faithful cross-cultural expressions of our Lutheran faith.

A second adaptation of worship in the inner-city congregation is greater participation by laypersons. In some congregations the laity not only serve as lectors, but under the direction of the pastor they may conduct any part of the service. Worship is as much an expression of the Christian faith of the whole congregation as any other part of life; it is not reserved solely for pastoral leadership. This is important in the city where worship should not be seen as separated from the life and struggles of its people.

In issues of church in society, urban congregations tend to have hands-on involvement. Many congregations, for example, may have discussion groups about apartheid in South Africa or letter-writing campaigns. In the inner city, it would be common to find members of local congregations who have participated in public demonstrations outside corporate headquarters. Many members of inner-city congregations help to organize and run food pantries or soup kitchens. This often involves people in coalitions with other churches and groups.

No single congregation, for example, can be as effective in maintaining a food pantry by itself as when it is part of an area-wide coalition. No one congregation can be as effective in bringing an issue before the city council as a coalition of congregations working together in support of one another. The ecumenical nature of the church further demands that congregations express their unity in as many ways as possible. It is of great importance for each congregation to decide which coalitions it wants to join—which coalitions best express the priorities for mission and ministry of that particular congregation.

Property management is an important component of urban ministry. The board of the local congregation responsible for the use and maintenance of the church properties should set guidelines for the use of the facilities by its own members and allow for maximum appropriate use by outside groups. In some neighborhoods the church is one of the few remaining places that can offer a meeting space for grass-roots groups, thus becoming a symbol of care and hope. A realistic and fair schedule of user fees for selected events should be established but, as already noted, most groups have few financial resources.

Program emphases will depend upon the demographics of the membership and the community. At Mt. Zion, for example, a large elderly membership and a strong interest in senior citizens' activities led to the formation of a Golden Age Club, which now has between eighty and ninety members. Meanwhile, a large number of community children from single-parent families needed more and better activities. The congregation responded by organizing a large summer youth program and Friday evening recreation program for primary school children. The Sunday school also has more children from the surrounding neighborhood than from families of congregational members. There is almost always need for a "singles" organization, which can be effectively developed through a coalition with other congregations. Organizations formed in inner-city churches will include members of different classes, races, or ethnic groups. These congregations, therefore, have an opportunity to develop integrated groupings which have not been common in the history of most mainline denominations.

Remaining in ministry in the inner city exacts a high cost from those who choose to make a long-term commitment. Why, then, do urban pastors stay?

As Lutherans, we believe that we offer a faithful and viable interpretation of the gospel which has meaning for the people of the inner city. Our Christian faith is tested by the challenge to care for the victims and the outcasts, and our ministry in turn opens up opportunities for the rest of the ELCA to respond as well. Our congregations provide service and advocacy, enjoying a unique opportunity to participate directly in the formation of public policy for the city. We urban pastors consider that our calling as Christians and as a church is to be faithful to the gospel, regardless of the consequences, within the difficult and often discouraging circumstances of inner-city ministry.

Today inner-city neighborhoods have become "foreign mission fields" as complex and challenging as any communities in the world. The church is an instrument of the hope, restoration, and community

Christ makes possible. As urban pastors and congregations, therefore, we seek God's guidance and blessing in all our efforts, knowing
that "except the Lord build . . . they that build, labor in vain. Except
the Lord keep watch over the city, the watchman watches in vain!"

CHAPTER **4**

Welcoming the Stranger

James R. Thomas

"As they came near the village to which they were going, he walked ahead as if he were going on. But they urged him strongly, saying, 'Stay with us, because it is almost evening and the day is now nearly over.' "

Luke 24:28-29

"Stay with us!" This was the invitation offered by two weakened disciples to one they took to be a stranger as they journeyed to the Judean town of Emmaus. Martin Luther called this petition of Cleopas and an unnamed companion "the prayer of good folk."[1] In this three word invitation, wrote Luther, "God permitted them to invite Christ, though they did not yet know that this was to be their salvation."[2] God visited the disciples clothed in the person of a stranger. The mode of visitation proved to be a surprise and a blessing.

Hospitality and salvation are linked in both testaments. My friend and teacher, John Koenig, correctly called attention to the central place that welcoming strangers has in the thoughts of several scriptural writers in his book, *New Testament Hospitality.*[3] Koenig notes that the three major festivals of the church—Christmas, Easter, and Pentecost—all have to do with the advent of a divine stranger. The newcomers offer blessings that cannot at first be comprehended. "The Child in the manger, the traveler on the road to Emmaus, and the mighty wind of the Spirit all meet us as mysterious visitors, challenging our belief systems even as they welcome us to new worlds."[4]

Kindness to strangers is noted by several writers in the Hebrew scriptures. For example, the writer of Exodus 23:9 warns: "You shall not oppress a resident alien; you know the heart of an alien, for you were aliens in the land of Egypt. Because God was Israel's host (Ps. 39:12; Lev. 25:23), Israel should therefore play host to others.[5]

The story of the widow of Zarephath can also be read profitably in this connection. In 1 Kings 17:8-16 we are introduced to a widow from the town of Zarephath who, after a demonstration of hospitality, learned the benefits of receiving strangers well. We are told that when this woman shared the last food she had with a stranger, she said, "That will be our last meal, and then we will starve to death" (1 Kings 17:12, TEV).

But Elijah, her guest, promised that her bowl of flour and her jar of oil would not run out before the day when the Lord would again send rain and provide food. The woman gave her last provisions to a stranger on the strength of God's promise made through her guest, Elijah. She soon discovered that entrusting oneself to God involves a risk of faith, and that life after will not be without tears.

Soon after her transaction with Elijah, her only son fell deathly ill. His death would be a great loss to his mother because he was an only child, and she would have no one to support her in her later years. The future looked grim for the widow. In her sorrow she wondered aloud why she was being tormented by Elijah. She questioned why God would deal so harshly with her. Had God sent Elijah to remind her of her sins?

Elijah, too, seemed mystified by the peril of the widow's son. In his prayers he cried out, "O Lord my God, why have you done such a terrible thing to this woman?" It was inconceivable to Elijah that after the widow's kindness to him, she should have to face the death of her child. After Elijah prayed for the stricken boy, he was revived. The widow exclaims, "Now I know that you are a man of God and that the Lord really speaks through you."

If the widow had treated her visitor with fear, suspicion, and distrust, she would very likely have missed a special visitation from God.

Hospitality to strangers involves welcoming something new and unknown into our lives. The ethicist Thomas Ogletree has observed that strangers have stories to tell that we have not heard before. These stories can redirect our seeing and stimulate our imaginations. The sharing of stories is not necessarily threatening, but may generate "a festive mood, a joy in celebrating the meeting of minds across social and cultural differences. The stranger does not simply challenge or subvert our assumed world of meaning; she may enrich, even transform, that world."[6]

Welcoming strangers! What a fitting description for the work of Christian congregations, not only in a large urban area such as New York City but in all places where the church is in mission and ministry. In small suburban communities and growing metropolitan centers, people are constantly on the move. The growing number of homeless people worldwide, brought on by poverty, unemployment, war, hunger, and other circumstances have made strangers of many.

In one way or another, all human beings need hospitality while they live on this earth. Many will experience care giving in hospitals, and they will be able to tell whether or not they were genuinely "cared for" or whether they were condescendingly being "taken care of."

Hundreds of thousands will line up during their lifetimes to eat meals served in soup kitchens. Some will be guests at grand hotels while others spend nights in shelters for the homeless. Some will know the kind of "hospitality" reserved for prisoners. A few travelers will catch sight of a "vacancy sign" late at night only to be turned away because they are not considered "average" or acceptable strangers. Sometimes we will be refused entry because of the color of our skin. Club membership may be determined by gender. A welcome sign alongside a set of high and imposing steps with no indication of handicap access will communicate some other message to the person in a wheelchair. The outcast, the pariah, the derelict— these forgotten people will not often find a warm welcome when they need a warm and safe habitation. Sadly, it will often be the one serving as "greeter" in a Christian congregation who erects the barriers to entrance.

During twelve years of ministry in New York City, in neigh-borhoods in the Bronx, Jamaica Queens, in Harlem, and on the Upper West Side of Manhattan, I came to know many strangers. Some wanted food. Others needed clothing. A few came with papers and needed assistance in gaining citizenship in the United States. I became acquainted with bag ladies and with men who regularly exchanged offerings given them from the pastor's discretionary fund and money received from panhandling for booze and drugs. These people, I was convinced, had needs that went far beyond their physical circumstances. Much of what Gustavo Gutierrez writes about poor and oppressed people in Latin America[7] is a fitting description of many on the streets of New York City. They, too, are robbed of the possibility of leading "fully human lives."[8] Gutierrez believes the battle between the nonbelievers and the religious world, which gave rise to a good deal of theology, does not speak to or express the experience of the poor. He says that the challenge does not come so much from the nonbeliever as it comes from the non-person. "It comes from the person whom the prevailing social order fails to recognize as a person—the poor, the exploited, the ones systematically and legally despoiled of their humanness, the ones who scarcely know that they are persons at all."[9]

While I was pastor of the Lutheran Church of the Advent, I was going to my bank, located beneath Madison Square Garden near the Pennsylvania Railroad Station. I was moving swiftly be-cause I had about three minutes to get into the door before the end of the banking day. Dressed in clericals, I belatedly realized that I would be targeted by many in need of a helping hand. While riding down on the Seventh Avenue escalator I saw a man standing at the foot of the moving stairs. I looked at his thin gaunt face and saw two bloodshot eyes encircled by black rings. Those eyes were win-dows to a soul long weakened by disappointment and discourage-ment. Failure was written upon his countenance. As people stepped off the escalator one by one, he seemed to look over their faces, perhaps for a smile or some other type of recognition. In some small way he was calling out, announcing to all of us, that he too was real and alive. As our eyes met I expected him to ask for help. I knew that if I stopped, he would start telling me a long story. In New York, it sometimes seems there is a logical progression followed by many in need. First you must hear the story of how the stranger arrived at his or her predicament. Then, and only then, will there be a request for help.

"Father," he said, "can I speak with you a moment?" I said, "I am sorry, sir, but I am on an errand of mercy and if I don't get into that bank in three minutes I am going to be in a great deal of trouble." I stepped away from the man and resumed my journey to the bank. As I walked on my way I heard these words from the stranger, "You call yourself a priest of God? Nigger, you ain't no priest! You ain't s--t!" I turned swiftly around and saw the amused faces of seventy or eighty commuters. I wanted to tell that man so much. I wanted to speak of my ordination at Our Saviour Church in the Bronx eleven years before. I felt like telling him about my work with homeless people while I was pastoring at Mount Zion Church in Harlem. I wished to tell him about how much I cared. Instead, I walked over to him and asked him to call me in one hour at my office. I gave him my card and a quarter and walked shame-facedly away. I assumed that the transaction was over.

When I returned to my office, the phone was ringing. Yes, it was my new acquaintance. He asked for an appointment. I invited him to come to my office the next day at 10:30 A.M. I arrived at 11:00 A.M. due to subway delays, but when I stepped out of the Ninety-sixth Street station onto Broadway there he was, pacing up and down in front of the church. I invited him in. While we moved toward the office I reached into my pocket and brought up five dollars. His first words upon seeing the money were "I want no money. Father, I just need to talk to somebody. I need to talk to you." He said that many people think that, just because he has his hand out, all he wants is money. He recalled that he once was doing well. He had a job. "I was fired due to technology." His company had "pink slipped" him a year ago because he could not operate the new equipment. "Father, I gave those SOBs fourteen years of my life. I had a pension shaping up. Is it right that they expect so much from a man who never finished elementary school?" he asked.

For several years I had kept an active referral file. I had just pulled out a folder when I heard him say, "I am not interested in being sent nowhere." "Well, how can I help you?" I asked. "Father, you can tell me what God has to say about my situation," he replied.

The stranger had come to talk about God. I had thought that he wanted something else.

I met my new acquaintance for several months in scheduled office visits. During our meetings I learned much of his personal history. He was very interested in the Bible and seemed to relate his life story to the parable of the prodigal son. One Sunday morning he surprised me with a visit to worship. That was the only time I saw him in church. One day he missed an appointment, and I worried and wondered about him for four months. Then one day he called and told me that he had found a new job. The pay was low, but that was no problem. My friend thanked me for helping him understand that the transitory events of his life did not add up to abandonment by God. He thanked me for welcoming him into my busy day. He said that our brief visits had helped him on the road to recovery as a full human being.

When I met the stranger I was going to the bank to withdraw funds for one in need. His entrance into my day provided one of the richest distractions in my ministry. He helped me understand something I had preached about for eleven years, namely, that we cannot close our eyes and our hearts and resources, nor abandon people who have very special needs.

I was very happy that the stranger called out to me. Without expecting it, I received help in being a pastor. He taught me not to pull out the "referral" file every time someone came into my office. I became a better listener. I learned that many people earnestly want to address the spiritual dimensions of their lives when they come to the church for help. It would be well for Christian care givers to learn how to "move toward" the stranger, as the father in Luke's parable moved toward the prodigal. Like the prodigal son, many people are trying to find the way home. They know why they have chosen the church rather than a social-service agency. Going to church is, for many, like going home.

There are many implications for ministry when we take seriously the biblical call for hospitality. As John Koenig writes, ". . . the kingdom perpetuates itself by growing up in its guests and coming to birth in their ministry as hosts." [10] We should make every effort in our parishes to build programs of welcome which assure visitors that "here" a stranger can find a home away from home. Such programs may include fellowship hours, a kind of continuation of the eucharistic meal. Perhaps it is in the fellowship hours that we can recapture some of the spirit of the early Christian community which gathered regularly in homes for the praise of God, mutual exhortation, and "the breaking of the bread."[11] These fellowship hours provide fertile ground for sharing stories, announcing important family transitions, and getting acquainted. Here we should also give special attention to the table. Coffee is no invitation to those who may not wish to drink coffee. Within our congregations there may be potential for providing nutritional foods from north, south, east and west. In an effective fellowship program, members can provide well-planned tables. It is also a sad fact that one of these meals may be the most food a guest will eat all week!

Betty, a twenty-nine-year-old homeless person, was a frequent guest at our fellowship hours. Betty had often visited in the pastor's office before she began to attend worship. Sometimes she would stay away for weeks and then, suddenly, as if she had an appointment, she would come in asking for shelter from the "grizzly and grotesque" people in the streets. One Sunday at coffee hour, Betty told me that she found Advent to be a friendly church but that when it came to the food we served our guests at fellowship hour, "you are quite cheap." She added, "I find that the food served at Holy Name Catholic Church on Ninety-sixth Street and Amsterdam Avenue is better for you." According to Betty, Advent served too much coffee and cake. At Holy Name they served fruit and juices. There were also cooked and raw vegetables on their table. Sometimes they even served sandwiches. "One got the impression that the people at Holy Name Church really cared about what they were serving you," she said. That, to Betty, could only mean that they cared about her. We were reminded that often there were things on our table which would never be served to guests in our homes. Betty, the stranger, had zeroed in on a small detail. Although Advent does from time to time provide splendid meals at fellowship time, it is the occasional stranger who may catch us at our worst. We learned from that experience to prepare more carefully for coffee hour.

Bible studies are also enhanced by planning that takes into account the personal journeys of those who make up the group. Members who grew up in Mississippi, or Iowa, people who were born and lived in Ghana or El Salvador: all these people have stories to tell. The actor might recall how he was converted when he had the role of Jesus Christ in an Easter play. Many of the so-called "street people" will begin to share when they notice that we will not shrink back when we hear something we do not understand. One such couple became regular members of Advent Church. At some point they began to bring food to our meetings, and we saw a transition from guests to host and hostess. Thomas Ogletree makes a useful observation about why we ought to hear the story of the stranger: "My readiness to welcome the other into my world must be balanced by my readiness to enter the world of the other. My delight in the stories of the other as enrichment for my orientation to meaning must be matched by my willingness to allow my own stories to be incorporated into the values and thought modes of the other." [12]

In planning worship we would also benefit from the insights of the newcomer. How many times have Lutheran congregations in changing neighborhoods simply ignored the arrival of new people! The hymns sung at worship reminded us of a Christianity rooted in Europe. The reconstructed ancient worship rites were adequate for the older membership, but the new arrivals would find little to satisfy their need for songs and stories that spoke to them. There were no bridges built to a growing Hispanic community. It was assumed that the African, the Asian, and the Native American now in our congregation had no interest in telling their own stories. The Christian experience was filtered through the lenses of white people. We droned on with our heavy German chorales and Anglo-American sectarian hymns while a changing world groaned for the help we refused to share. In refusing, we missed the blessings.

On the first Easter, Cleopas and his companion invited Christ to spend the night with them, but during the evening meal the roles were reversed. The disciples had offered the invitation, but it was Jesus who presided at the table. "When he was at table with them, he took bread, blessed and broke it, and gave it to them. Then their eyes were opened, and they recognized him" (Luke 24:30-31a). As Christ opened up the Scriptures to the disciples, they were able to recognize him. Not until they received the stranger and allowed him the freedom to share were their eyes opened. Frederick W. Danker notes the fact that this stranger, Jesus, longed to continue communication with his disciples. "But only those who desire his company will come to further realization of his identity." [13]

Christians are called to identify the presence of Christ among the sick and in jails among the convicted. People in poverty, those who make up a despised class, persons suffering from oppression, people at war in churches and doing battle in their workplaces and in the public square: these, too, we must greet as though we were welcoming Jesus Christ. To invite people in, to offer them security and comfort, to remember them when we pray, to help them with deeds of kindness: all of this is to recall Christ. It is, as Martin Luther said, hearing the voice of Christ crying out to us from another's body.

As we open our doors and our hearts to others, we must be genuine in our actions and intent. Cleopas and his companion invited the stranger willingly, out of kindness, just as their teacher would have done for them. For it was Christ who had identified with them when they needed so much. It was Christ who had placed himself alongside them and had taken on their burdens. Now, through a small deed of loving-kindness to a stranger, Christ had identified himself fully to them . . . and with them.

CHAPTER **5**

Outreach in an Urban Setting

John Milbrath

Throughout the United States there are hundreds of urban congregations that were built several decades ago in growing neighborhoods. These neighborhoods have gone through an aging process, and the congregations located in such neighborhoods have also aged. Along with the aging of the congregations and neighborhoods, there has often been a decline in Sunday school participation, in church membership, and in attendance at worship. These declines are normal because of the changing population of the neighborhood surrounding the church. They are also painful and not fully understood by the local membership.

Bethany Lutheran Church of Portland, Oregon, is a congregation like hundreds of other city congregations in the Evangelical Lutheran Church in America. In the 1950s it experienced rapid growth due to its location near new home construction and to the postwar boom. Eventually the neighborhood aged and so did the congregation, experiencing first a leveling off of growth and then a decline during the sixties and seventies.

When an aging neighborhood reaches a certain point, it begins to recycle. Homes recently owned by retired widows or widowers are sold, and most often purchased by younger persons, sometimes families with children. This means that, once again, there is a growing mission field in the neighborhood where the church building is located. The field is more scattered than in new suburban missions, but it is nevertheless an important field for mission. Congregations located in these neighborhoods are in an excellent position for mission outreach to the new residents. Many such parishes have adequate buildings, often fully paid for. The congregations have the stability of long existence in the area, and usually have the good will and trust of the community. They have a membership that, if properly encouraged, is able to assist in the mission outreach to the neighborhood. Such congregations are in a unique position because they often have older citizens within their membership who can advise and evaluate the service that is being attempted, and because they often possess a core of volunteers who have time and energy to carry out programs of service to the community.

Aging congregations, however, tend to have a negative image of themselves because they have lost membership over the years. Such discouragement must be remedied so that it does not impair evangelization of the neighborhood.

Convinced that there still was a mission field in their neighborhood, the three hundred confirmed members of Bethany Lutheran congregation began planning their outreach approach in 1980 under the leadership of Pastor Norman A. Dahle. After much discussion, it was agreed that there is so much legitimate ministry to the needs of older members in an aging parish that the pastor has little time left to be a mission developer for the recycling neighborhood. Thus, it became obvious that a second pastor was required. The second staff person would have the specific task of "outreach into the community." The idea hardly sounds new, but we did not find any examples in our North Pacific District of the former American Lutheran Church (ALC). What we proposed was a model that attempted to reestablish a new ministry in a suburban area. In a time when suburban growth had slowed in many cities and when the cost of starting new package missions had skyrocketed, the reestablishment of "mission" in an existing parish was a timely idea.

Bethany Lutheran congregation accepted this model for itself early in 1980 and worked consistently toward its goal. The Bethany Outreach Project became a reality in mid-1982, when a seed grant of $30,000 was given by the ALC's Division of Service and Mission in America, to help in calling an "Outreach Pastor." The model had two components. The first was the calling of a full-time staff member for the specific task of evangelistic outreach in the parish and its neighborhood. Pastor John A. Milbrath was called to that position in July of 1982, joining Pastor Norman A. Dahle on the pastoral staff.

The second part of the model was to enlarge the definition of outreach to include a broad spectrum of service to the community. The parish was committed to the vision and task of outreach to the whole person. A parish so deeply involved in wholistic service could not help but create within itself a climate favorable to the reception of new people from the neighborhood. Therefore, Bethany congregation has defined evangelism as applying the gospel to the hearts of our fellow human beings, winning the unsaved for Christ, recalling the backsliders to Christ, keeping the believers strongly rooted in Christ, and sending the believers out to be witnesses for Christ. These are not periodic or separable activities of the congregation. Rather, the whole congregation must be permeated with a spirit of scriptural evangelism, which also involves wholehearted, unreserved service to our neighbors in the community.

There have been three primary ways our outreach ministry has worked to serve the community. The first has addressed the outreach pastor's responsibility to the large number of retired people among Bethany's membership. A great deal of time has been spent in individual counseling with the grieving and the depressed. I have helped people secure legal assistance and necessary tax help. I have attended court with individuals, helped with shopping, gone along to the doctor's office for moral support, and assisted with funeral prearrangements. I have screened retirement homes, nursing homes, and adult foster-care homes, and have helped to select and move several people into appropriate facilities. I have attempted to stay informed about the availability of government help in securing new furnaces, storm windows, and other energy-saving modifications. Several persons have qualified for low-cost improvements on their older homes. Any of these problems can become weighty burdens for our retired members, especially for elderly persons who live alone. As a natural response to this concern for older people, Bethany congregation has related itself to a local retirement home, where worship services are held one Sunday afternoon each month by the Bethany pastors.

The second main area of outreach also serves the retired people of our parish and neighborhood. This is primarily a social program of group activities designed to promote fellowship and build new friendships. A strong core group of "young" retired people at Bethany do a wonderful job of keeping things lively and incorporating the elderly into the fun. Once a month there is a community potluck gathering, which is well attended by Bethany Church members and friends from the neighborhood. Lunch is sometimes followed by a brief program. Occasionally outside speakers have led discussions on topics such as nutrition and alcoholism. Sometimes group members have volunteered to present programs such as travelogues. On another day each month, we charter a bus and take a trip. Costs are kept as low as possible and a variety of activities are included. Longer trips have also been included on the agenda. In planning these outings, we take advantage of the wealth of interesting attractions and activities in our own city as well as the great natural beauty of our region. Both the monthly trips and the potluck gatherings at the church have contributed greatly to the general morale of the congregation. We have seen a new spirit and hope in many of our older members. A number of people have been revitalized through new interests, friendships, and frequent contacts with others in the parish.

The third major way our outreach program has served the community involves linking parish members to service organizations already functioning in the community. This is, by far, the most involved and extensive branch of our program.

During my first three months as outreach pastor, I spent a great deal of time getting acquainted with my new parish. I asked questions and listened. I discovered that there were many people in the parish who were committed to working regularly with local charities and service groups. These activities outside the congregation had never been recognized as "church mission work." It seemed to me that any such work, done in the spirit of Christian love by any member of a parish, should be recognized as an outreach extension of that parish. Generally these people did not want to be appointed to a "church committee" as such. They were willing to talk with others in the parish about their charitable projects, however only in an effort to enlist additional volunteers. These people formed the first of our "outreach teams," whose responsibility it was to coordinate congregational activities with various social-service groups in the city. Seven years into the program, we now have thirty-four such outreach teams of one-to-four persons each, performing very specific functions. For example, one team secures volunteers for the Meals on Wheels and Loaves and Fishes programs. Another team keeps in contact with the large Alcoholics Anonymous group that meets weekly in our church building. Another team works with Tough Love, a parent-youth drug counseling group, and Grant Area Free from Drug Abuse (GAFFDA), a parent drug counseling group. These last two groups have met periodically in our building.

Hospice care, job counseling, coordinating volunteer services for senior citizens in Portland are among the many areas of involvement. Some members of our parish perform valuable services such as shopping, minor home repairs, yard work, and providing transportation and companionship for elderly neighbors. Yet another team works with Marriage Encounter, and one heads a Transportation Committee within the parish. A team cooperates with the local Neighborhood Association in solving problems in the immediate area surrounding the church. Today that includes the growing impact of youth gangs upon our community. The Neighborhood Association, in connection with the Portland Police Bureau, regularly conducts Crime Prevention Seminars in our church.

A disability team has made our church building totally accessible by the addition of two wheelchair ramps, one into the sanctuary and one into the basement, and by altering our restrooms. Our weekly church bulletins and monthly newsletters are printed in enlarged type for the visually impaired.

Another team works with Northwest Pilot Project, a local housing group that locates and helps finance low-cost housing for the homeless in our city. One team actively participates in the task of alleviating hunger through the Sunshine Division of the Portland Police Bureau. This team keeps the membership advised about what food and clothing items are most needed. Our food and clothing barrels fill up weekly, and all donations are put to immediate use. There is an outreach team linked with the Boys and Girls Aid Society of Oregon. A group of young unmarried mothers meets regularly in our church with the Boys and Girls Aid Society staff members to learn child-care skills and to receive emotional and social support.

Bethany's outreach program also relates to the Red Cross. One outreach team has organized a blood pressure screening clinic, operated by Red Cross nurses, in our building. This service is offered twice each month and free of charge to all citizens of the neighborhood. Our building is also used by the Red Cross to hold various classes for the community. These include: baby-sitting safety skills for youngsters aged eleven and above, home nursing skills, and a body signals course designed to teach people to measure their own blood pressure.

Our congregation has become aware also of the critical needs of a local service agency called the "Greenhouse" (so named because former Oregon Congresswoman Edith Green was instrumental in founding the agency, and continues to be a chief supporter). The Greenhouse operates a building in the heart of downtown Portland that serves as a support center for homeless street children. Dedicated staff members and volunteers struggle to meet the daily needs of children and teenagers, providing hot meals, clothing, blankets, medical care, companionship, and emotional support. Several Bethany members are regularly involved in preparing and donating complete meals for the Greenhouse kitchen.

Linking their volunteer efforts with existing social service agencies, a growing number of Bethany's members are now working actively in direct service to others. Each year, on the third Sunday in November, we celebrate an annual Outreach Fair. After the first year of the outreach program, we learned that good communication was vital to success. A forum was needed in which our entire membership could gain firsthand knowledge of the work of the outreach teams. The Outreach Fair was created to answer this need, and has evolved into the annual meeting of the outreach program. For this event, the parish hall is decorated in a festive Thanksgiving motif. Each outreach team sets up a small booth that visually describes its activities during the past year. After a potluck dinner, the chairperson of each team gives a brief report. The directors of the social service agencies with which we are affiliated are given an opportunity to speak.

It has become increasingly obvious to our membership that the more we do for our less-fortunate neighbors, the more we are made aware of other areas where help is desperately needed. Many agency administrators who have attended our fair have reported that, besides enjoying the cooking, they have found our forum to be helpful in practical ways. For example, when one service agency expresses a critical need for beds and mattresses, and another agency represented in the group has an excess of beds and mattresses stored in a warehouse, a serious problem is solved instantly. Administrative heads of local service agencies are eager to attend our fair because they report that they receive much useful information about services offered by other agencies. This information is extremely valuable in a large city where it is often necessary to refer people with specific needs to agencies equipped to handle those particular problems.

Prior to a recent Outreach Fair, the Red Cross issued an urgent citywide appeal for blood donations. On the same weekend as our fair, therefore, our church building was used for a community blood drive. This will be an annual event, in connection with each Outreach Fair, to emphasize the giving, sharing aspect of outreach.

The greatest new challenge facing us is the development of a ministry to the Southeast Asian population of Portland. During the years since 1974, a great number of Southeast Asian immigrants have made Portland their home. Their presence and culture have had a significant impact on our city. Some time ago, a dedicated layperson in our parish, an employee of a Vietnamese businessman, came to the pastors at Bethany with an exciting story. His employer, Mr. Phan Cong Van, who grew up in a Christian family in Vietnam and immigrated to Portland twelve years ago, has since his arrival been serving as lay pastor to a small, struggling group of Vietnamese Christians. Many of these immigrants were sponsored by Lutheran congregations, and felt a certain identity with Lutheranism.

Lay Pastor Van and his congregation were aware of the development of the first Vietnamese Lutheran congregation in the United States, located in Seattle, Washington. After a great deal of discussion, this local group determined that it wanted to pursue affiliation with the former American Lutheran Church. Using the Seattle congregation as a model, the first steps were taken toward that goal. The first Sunday of January 1987 seemed an appropriate time for that new beginning. The Vietnamese congregation used our church facility for the first time on that day, and thirty-five people attended an afternoon worship service. Attendance has increased on each successive Sunday, and people have come from many sections of the city. Lay Pastor Van officiates at the services, reading the liturgy and preaching in his native language. The two Bethany pastors alternate in attending the Vietnamese worship services, where they administer the sacraments and give any help and support that is needed. Pastor John Dovinh of the Seattle Vietnamese Lutheran congregation gave encouragement, and provided invaluable assistance by supplying us with his Vietnamese language translation of the communion service from the *Lutheran Book of Worship (LBW)*.

As a possible extension of our assistance to the Southeast Asian community, we are now conducting a feasibility study for the development of a preschool in our church building. The purpose of such a school would be to help prepare young Southeast Asian children for their entrance into the public school system. It would operate in conjunction with the Vietnamese congregation and serve as an evangelistic branch of that ministry. Space for such a program is available in our facility. We at Bethany congregation are determined to continue our support for this ministry with and for Vietnamese people.

We have been given a wealth of spiritual, material, and human resources that we gladly dedicate to the renewal of the wider community. Sharing, giving, and caring are essential in the community-building process. That process must begin on a personal level with lives unselfishly committed to serving others. With Christ's love as its model, Bethany congregation has set its course according to John 15:16: "You did not choose me but I chose you. And I appointed you to go and bear fruit, fruit that will last." Our church's vocation is to walk in the footsteps of Christ.

The results of our outreach program have been evident from the beginning. During the six-month period immediately preceding the inception of the program (January-June 1982), the average attendance at Sunday worship services was 145. Eighteen months into the program, during those same months in 1984, average attendance rose to 177. Sunday school enrollment and financial giving were also up by a slightly smaller percentage. Since 1984, membership has increased by about 4 percent annually. Bethany's sharp decline in the years 1965 to 1975, and the plateau between 1975 and 1982, seemed to be reversing. Growth in worship attendance has again leveled off, largely because of street gangs. A comparison with similarly placed congregations in our city and elsewhere shows a similar pattern. The biggest change has occurred in the congregation's perception of its role in the wider community. It has truly become an outreach-oriented, service-minded group of people.

Our work is a faithful local expression of the church's age-long mission to bring Christ's love to a world of suffering and despair. We share the vision of the ancient biblical writer who saw that "See, the home of God is among mortals. He will dwell with them as their God; they will be his peoples, and God himself will be with them; he will wipe every tear from their eyes. Death will be no more; mourning, and crying and pain will be no more, for the first things have passed away" (Rev. 21:3-4).

C H A P T E R **6**

Transfiguration Lutheran Church

Heidi Neumark

To describe the mission and ministry of Transfiguration Lutheran Church/Iglesia Luterana de la Transfiguración, I would like to tell about a typical Sunday morning with this congregation in the South Bronx. Use your imagination in order to move with me through the morning. Without imagination, ours, but most of all God's, there would be no Sunday at Transfiguration worth telling about.

8:00 A.M. As you approach the church the first thing you will see are the street-level front doors painted brightly with a scene from this day's gospel. Across the top of the doors is a verse from the text painted in both English and Spanish.

The doors have been painted during the previous week by a group of neighborhood youth. Each week they meet, read the lesson, think and talk about what images come to mind that they would like to use. They select the verse and set about the task of painting the doors. Through this process the youth discover that they are not only recipients of the gospel, but that they themselves can give shape and color to the good news.

There is good Lutheran precedent for the use of doors to proclaim what we believe! There we post our theses for all to see: the gospel belongs to this neighborhood! The good news is present here! These doors welcome God's family gathered here. People notice our doors and often stop to speak about them. The doors speak back.

Three years ago, the doors were graffiti-covered and locked six days a week. It had not always been so. Transfiguration began about fifty-five years ago in Manhattan, established by the Caribbean Synod to serve Spanish-speaking Lutherans who had moved from Puerto Rico to New York. Twenty years later, the church moved to the South Bronx, following its members. Those were thriving years for the church of more than five hundred baptized members. At the time, Transfiguration was the Spanish language Lutheran church in New York City.

Then came the 1960s and devastation in the South Bronx. Many of the church's members, working middle-class people, were able to move out of the immediate neighborhood to other more stable areas of the Bronx. They began commuting to church. In time, some moved farther away. Others died. Children grew up and began their families elsewhere. After the forty-year pastorate of the Rev. Jaime Soler ended, no pastor remained in the congregation for much more than two years. There were lengthy vacancy periods and one part-time ministry. Before I accepted a call to the congregation, it had been without a pastor for five years. A visiting pastor would come in on Sunday mornings.

During these years, little neighborhood evangelism was attempted. Pride in the church gave way to fear for the church. The inevitable result was a sharp decline in church membership and activities. And so, when I arrived, it was to greet a small group (about twenty-five) that gathered once a week behind locked doors. The fresh paint on the doors is thus a blazing signal of fresh direction for the church.

As we get close to the doors, you will see a child waiting there. Her name is Cristina and she is nine years old. Her mother is a drug addict who lives in Queens. Cristina lives in an apartment half a block from the church with her elderly grandmother and her father who has been in and out of treatment programs for drug and alcohol abuse.

Just as I am about to open the door another girl, Maria, comes around the corner. She is also nine and has lost both parents to drugs—one was a victim of AIDS, the other a victim of a gunshot. These two girls are involved in every activity at the church that they can be in—acolyte club, Sunday school, Homework Help, choir, and drama group. Both have been baptized and received Communion instruction at the church. The church is a haven for them and for many children.

We now go inside with Cristina and Maria. They want to help and there is plenty to be done. While I run off copies of hymn sheets, they get started folding the bulletin that we will use for the Spanish service.

8:30 A.M. Other helpers arrive along with Sharon, a twenty-two-year-old who has come to set up the altar with some of the acolytes. After three years, we still do not have a well-functioning altar guild for both services. There have been Sundays when I had to send one of the kids to the bodega on the corner to buy a white handkerchief so we could have a clean purificator. Sometimes this gets discouraging. There seem to be innumerable things to start, reform, and organize. It is impossible to see that it is all done at once, or even in three years. Virtually every area of parish life needs work, hard work, which translates into time. Not that I as pastor must or should do it all, but organizing and training others takes time too.

One thing that has been immeasurably helpful in making the best use of my time and energy and that of the congregation has been setting down an overall vision, some long-term goals and some priorities each year. Living in a neighborhood that operates on day-to-day crisis and survival, it is easy, and deadly, to fall into the same pattern. I have worked with this process of vision, goals, and priorities both personally with a colleague and together with the church council.

Of course, some unexpected situations call for an immediate response. While it has taken three years to find some important church records, it was only within hours of my arrival that I noticed a box of rat poison kept under the altar right next to a box of communion wafers. This situation was immediately remedied without resorting to any discussion or vote. I had nightmares of picking up the wrong box after a particularly late Saturday night and consecrating the wrong elements.

8:45 A.M. Two more people come through the doors, Clarissa and Pastor John Augustine. Clarissa has come to make breakfast and John has come to make photocopies of his Sunday bulletin on the machine we share. Neither of our churches could afford to buy a copy machine on our own, but together we were able to make the purchase. Such cooperation is essential to effective ministry.

In addition to sharing a copy machine, John and I are part of a coalition of Lutheran churches, South Bronx ministry. As in many urban coalitions, the pastors and interns meet weekly for Bible study, discussion, and evaluation of our ministries. Occasional guests help us to explore topics such as evangelism. We also are involved in a number of joint programs such as the basketball league, sharing a summer beach house, and training for lay leaders. An important recent action of the coalition has been the formation of a Neighborhood Development Corporation (NDC) to raise funds for a variety of parish-based programs. Through the NDC, we at Transfiguration have been able to provide job counseling and placement, drug counseling and an improved after school program.

By now Clarissa is in the kitchen putting bread into the oven. She is new in the church. Her five children were part of last year's summer program. Clarissa, like many persons, came to the church at a point of transition in her life—having just left an abusive husband. In the church, Clarissa has found others to share in her struggle toward a new life. Her children, particularly the three oldest (ages twelve, thirteen, and fourteen), are having a very difficult time after years of abuse. The oldest now lives in a group home and visits his family on the weekends. In our congregation, shut-in visits include group homes such as the one this boy is in, Rikers Island Prison and Spotford, a nearby juvenile detention center.

9:00 A.M. Clarissa prepares a breakfast for our Sunday school of orange juice and nutritious, tasty breads baked by the women's group of a suburban church with whom we have a partnership. Many of the children have no other breakfast on the weekend since school is closed. This simple meal, served between 9:00 and 9:30, helps them get through the morning. It also helps get some of the kids to Sunday school on time.

9:30 A.M. "It's me, it's me, it's me, O Lord. . . ." Sunday school begins with group singing, an offering, and a prayer. Then the classes divide up. Three years ago, there was no Sunday school for youth. In fact, on my first Sunday, the only child in the church was the granddaughter of one older member. We now have fifty children and youth who participate in Sunday school. Our building is small and in order to accommodate them we have to make additional classroom space by moving pews in the sanctuary.

At first, Sunday school classes were taught by me, seminary students, and later an intern. Now, all the classes, except the teenagers, are taught by new members from the neighborhood. One of the teachers, Deloras, who began by feeling very tentative and insecure about herself and her skills, initiated a project to reorganize all our church-school materials. Then she went on to organize a workshop of Sunday school teachers in other Lutheran churches. She will receive our Teacher of the Year award at the annual Sunday school teachers Recognition Dinner held by the Bronx Lutheran churches. Deloras and her leadership skills are blossoming. She has gotten off welfare and, with the assistance of our jobs counselor, has found a job at a day-care center.

One challenge we face in our Sunday school, a challenge faced by many urban churches, is choice of materials. Or rather, lack of choice. The materials published by the national church seldom work in our setting. Geared for white, middle-class congregations, most materials are of little use in the South Bronx.

But it is possible for the church to change this situation. When I was in South America, where I completed my last year of seminary, I was deeply impressed by a decision made by the Roman Catholic diocesan office in Lima, Peru. They decided that instead of coming out with new resources every year for the middle-class churches, which already had more curricula than they needed, they would focus their entire budget on the needs of poor communities who had gone for years receiving only the scraps from the table of educational materials. Those poor communities worked with the diocesan staff to produce new materials that would actually be useful to poor communities. It's time for that dream in the ELCA!

10:00 A.M. Sunday school is now well under way. I am checking to make sure that everything is ready for our English worship. The fact that an English service is about to begin is in itself a major change for Transfiguration, a change that reflects the makeup of our neighborhood.

The population is about 65 percent Hispanic and 35 percent black. The once purely hispanic congregation now includes black sisters and brothers with their language, culture, and music. Thus, an English service.

Our average attendance in the English service has now grown to between fifty-five and sixty. Children and teenagers outnumber adults. This partly reflects the demographic reality of our neighborhood. It also reflects the fact that many of our children come from the most unstable family situations. Many parents are addicted to drugs or alcohol. Many are depressed, unable to get up the energy to go to the laundromat or send the kids to school, much less attend church regularly. Some examples:

Four of our nine-year-old girl acolytes were sexually abused by a man with the consent of their mothers to whom he gave drugs and other "gifts" in exchange for time with their daughters. I do not consider myself a social worker, but I spent quite a bit of time in the Distrist Attorney's office and in court with the girls to make sure that this man would be off our streets permanently. It's part of what it takes to keep the wolves away from the flock.

Chenise, the girl who played Mary in our 1986 Three Kings play, was given away by her mother to a team of Jehovah's Witnesses who just came to the door of the apartment where her mother, Linda, was temporarily staying with a friend. Linda had never seen these Witnesses before but thought that she couldn't cope with her daughter any more and keep trying to find housing. The friend she was staying with, Debra, who belonged to the church with her three children, has since had to move into a shelter for battered women in another borough.

Zoraida had come to church once for a baptism and had never returned. Then one Sunday a year later, she showed up saying that she was "going through a change." I could see from the wasted look on her face and body what the change was. She had become addicted to heroin. Zoraida came because she wanted help. We had no drug counselor at the time, but I was able to get her into a hospital. When she came out, she began attending Narcotics Anonymous meetings at the church on Monday nights. She came to a Bible study and became a member. It was wonderful to see Zoraida slowly emerging from her prison of anguish into a new life with her three children. Then one night, the husband she had kicked out when he wouldn't kick his habit broke into her apartment and almost killed her in front of the children. Her teenage daughter tried to commit suicide. They fled to a relative in New Jersey and I have never seen or heard from them again.

Our neighborhood is filled with this violence, suffering, and instability. Now, so is our church. It has taken time, teaching, and firsthand experience, but now almost all of our older members understand why some of our children have trouble concentrating and controlling themselves. There is room at the table for those who squirm, laugh inappropriately, and even fight. Within the chalice there is grace enough for all.

One step forward has been simply keeping our doors open to the injustice and pain that rages through our streets. The second step, that inevitably had to follow, has been to seek more ways to bring healing to this place. The drug and job counselors and after school staff that we have through the NDC are one such means. With them, our ministry with the families in our community is more complete. In addition, we have just started another program called Mothers Arise or Madres en Pie especially for women who are walking the fine line between just hanging on and losing control completely. We hope that through this program, the women will find the support and skills they need to build a decent life for themselves and their children. We also hope that their eyes will be opened to see that they are valued beyond price, made in God's holy image, with a future full of promise. One day, through these ministries, as well as others, we hope to have as many adults as youth filling the pews during our English worship.

10:30 A.M. Sunday school is over and we have fifteen minutes to get ready for the English worship. I have to get vested, as do the worship assistants and acolytes. We use as many acolytes as possible because it gives them a chance to take a visible, important part in worship leadership. It enables children and youth who have often felt that they don't count for much to realize that they are precious in the eyes of the Lord and in the functioning of their church. This is also time for all the kids to go to the bathroom before worship begins so that there is no distracting running in and out later on. The only two toilets we have are in a very narrow hallway through which the adults arriving for Spanish Sunday school must squeeze along with the anxious crowds waiting to use the toilets. This is one of many reasons that we need more space.

Among the adults now coming into the church is Joanne. It wasn't until a family crisis that Joanne became really active in the church. Her sister Lorraine and her brother-in-law Joe had a baby who died of AIDS contracted through a blood transfusion. They had once been Baptist, but had not been attending church for years. They had no pastor. Joanne asked me to go to the funeral home and pray. I went and was amazed, after Scripture readings and prayers, to see the entire immediate family, including the grieving mother, stand up and sing their hearts out. Rich, strong gospel notes encircled the room gathering the family, and me with them, back to the dusty roads and green fields of North Carolina where they grew up. I understood how that mother could sing through her pain. She was singing her way home.

Not long after this, Lorraine, Joe, Joanne, and her children became members of the church. The children were baptized that Easter. Since that time, they have formed a gospel chorus to sing us home during communion each week. They sang "Wade in the Water" at our daughter Ana's baptism. It meant a lot having waded with them through the tears and risen up in resurrection hope at little Tawana's death.

10:45 A.M. The bells are ringing. Now imagine that you are entering the sanctuary. To your immediate right is the baptismal font whose waters have had little rest recently. When I arrived at Transfiguration, I discovered the font, after some searching, pushed into a corner at the back of the church along with some objects that were kept there for occasional use. One of these objects was a plastic Advent wreath. During Advent, the font served as a stand to hold the wreath. I was not kidding when I said it had to be dusted off. Glory be to Jesus that locked doors, dusty fonts, and apartment buildings collapsed into a rubble of dry bones, do not deter his spirit from awakening, washing, and lifting us into the light of a new day.

Hanging above the font is a brightly colored wall-hanging from Haiti. Although we have no members from Haiti, the black Jesus is a welcome sign of the incarnation for our black sisters and brothers. The fruits ripening on the branches of the tree are easily recognized by other members as the blessings of a Caribbean paradise.

An even more brilliantly painted and significant mural hangs on another wall of the sanctuary. It was painted by the children and teenage tutors in our after school program under the direction of our intern who had led them in a study of God's presence in our neighborhood. This beautiful mural depicts the streets around our block with the church in the center proclaiming, "Love Thy Neighborhood." Children jumping double Dutch, fire hydrants, dogs, pigeons, bodegas, and apartment buildings are all clearly painted. But the radiant colors and harmonious activities of all the people infuse the scene with a heaven-sent glory. It is the South Bronx as the holy city of Revelation, the place where God is at home, where death and sadness, crack vials and bullets are no more, where no gates are locked for there is no night, and nothing unclean, and God's radiant glory is everywhere. This is what you see as you enter our sanctuary, even as the acolytes are dashing about in search of a match.

As worship begins, we do not open *LBW*s, but use photocopies from the *LBW* that allow us to change some of the music. For instance, we tried various tunes for the Agnus Dei and Sanctus until we found what was best for us. I knew we had hit upon a good Sanctus when a group of children came up to me during the sharing of the peace and asked, "Is it almost time to sing the Holy, Holy, Holy?"

Our hymnody includes black spirituals and gospel music, some "mainline" Protestant and *LBW* hymns, some modern folk-style hymns and a few songs from Africa and chants from Taizé. From this eclectic mixture we express the gospel and our faith. It is a lot of work to make seasonal liturgies each year and type out and copy all the hymns for two services each week (with no secretary), so we are in the process of preparing our own worship book. It will have three sections: Spanish, English, and bilingual.

Although we do a lot of teaching about worship in virtually all programs that involve children and youth and we try to celebrate

70

the full drama of each liturgical season, I sometimes wonder what gets through. But one day I entered the sanctuary to find two acolytes "playing church." I was amazed to see them begin with the confession and then move through a prayer, readings, sermon, prayers, peace, offering, Communion, and blessing. Somehow these two nine-year-olds who never seem to be paying attention, had gotten the basic shape of the liturgy.

11:45 A.M. English worship and Spanish Sunday school are now over and we all come together for refreshment and fellowship. I knew we were making progress when new members began to feel comfortable and welcome in the kitchen. In many churches I think that kitchen fellowship takes longer to achieve than altar fellowship. One thing that makes this between service time together a little less than refreshing is the crowdedness. We have been steadily outgrowing our space for fellowship as well as for teaching and programming. We have enough room because our worship is divided into two services, though on bilingual Sundays we are just about at our limit. That, however, is preferable than having a huge sanctuary where even 150 people seem to be a scattered handful.

Because of this happy space problem, we are engaging in a fund-raising campaign that will help us toward our goal of building into the parking lot. With the assistance of Lutheran Laity Movement (LLM) we set a top goal of $15,000 and a minimum goal of $10,000, over a three-year period. So far our pledges from members have reached almost $34,000 and we still have some more visits to go. It has been uplifting to see the shared sense of vision, mission, and investment in this campaign, which we call "Coming Together in Christ—to Grow in the Bronx." Those with jobs, those on welfare and fixed social-security incomes, new members, old members, people who are not yet members, blacks, Hispanics, young, and old have all truly come together. One woman, whom I expected might be able to contribute $1 a week at most, came to our treasurer last Sunday with $1,000 that she had received after her husband died. She said that she had been saving the money for something special. "This is the first time in my life that my money can make a difference" she said. The teenagers alone have pledged almost

$3,000 in weekly gifts that range from fifty cents to $2, which I might add they are bringing each Sunday.

I do not believe we will get the full amount that has been pledged, but it is only because some people's enthusiasm is bigger than their wallets will stand in the long run. In any case, we will certainly far exceed our initial goals. A partner church has pledged us their contribution of $50,000. That will still leave us with a mortgage of over $100,000. We are seeking guidance from the synod and national church, as well as the Holy Spirit, to make sure that as we go forward with this building, it will indeed free us for growth in mission and ministry and will not paralyze us with debt.

The unity that has been manifested in this campaign is what we seek to foster each week with the fellowship time between services. It is also the purpose of our annual retreat. At last year's retreat, we had an activity in which we were divided up into small groups. Each group included some people who speak only English and some who speak only Spanish. Each group was given a well-known Bible story in both languages with the instructions to read the story and figure out how they would act it out. They could choose from an array of props that were provided. There were only two rules. Everyone in each group had to participate in each drama and the dramas had to be performed without speech. When each group had had time to prepare, they presented their drama and the rest had to guess what story it was. In each case, it was abundantly clear what story was being told. The lesson: the good news was shared and language differences did not get in the way. This is, of course, the living drama we present as a bilingual congregation.

I have felt that it is essential for us to be one congregation with two languages rather than two different bodies meeting in one building. While our neighborhood is filled with churches, I know of none that have gone in this direction. There are many reasons to focus energy and resources on being a black or Hispanic congregation, but we have discovered gospel grace in being united. It is possible that this choice has slowed down our growth in numbers (I am not sure), but I do know that other priceless growth has occurred. To see some of the elderly Hispanic women and some of the teenage boys, fresh off the streets, reach the point of knowing each other by name and talking with each other is for me such a pearl without price. I'll never forget the Sunday when Juanita, a frail, elderly woman who had been initially frightened by some of the rambunctious new blood in the church, came and told me of a problem that Ricky had confided in her. These flashes of seeing that "water is thicker than blood," as the Rev. Richard Perry said in a recent sermon in the Bronx, encourage me to feel that we have made the right choice.

12:15 P.M. The acolytes ring the bells that signal the beginning of our Spanish service.

Since we have no sacristy, Victor and I are vesting in my little office. Victor is our council president, a young man of unusual commitment and faith. Victor will be my worship assistant along with the intern in the Spanish service. His attendance at both services each week is a great support to me and a wonderful way for him to get to know and be known by all our members. While we vest, I check a couple of verb tenses and other words that I might have difficulty with in my Spanish sermon. Victor is also the treasurer of our Neighborhood Development Corporation and has gone to Industrial Areas Foundation (IAF) national training as a leader in South Bronx churches. Since Victor has returned from training, our council meetings begin on time to the minute and no one, except for me on one embarrassing occasion, has ever come late again. He runs the meeting with an expertise appreciated by all. Since the training, Victor has initiated personal visits to all new members.

Luisa and Carmen are arriving with four hyperactive children who have been in and out of the hospital with lead poisoning. Carmen, their mother, is someone we would love to get involved with Madres en Pie, but so far this has not happened. Others are missing. Aurora, eighty-one years old, is in the hospital with pneumonia because the heat is not working in her city-run apartment building. Altagracia is another victim of the housing shortage. When her sister moved, she had to leave the apartment too. After staying with friends for seven months and looking for an apartment she could afford on her factory salary, she became pregnant and moved into a welfare hotel. After the baby was born, she was placed in an apartment in Manhattan. Altagracia visits once in a while, but will never be a part of our congregational life as she was when she lived a half-block away. In all I can count twelve families that we have lost over a three-year period because of problems related to housing. This is one of the reasons our participation in South Bronx churches is so vital, with our plan of housing construction. Knowing this will happen makes the present situation of powerlessness a little more bearable as more families become homeless.

Most of our worshipers have now arrived. The number is about the same as in the first service, giving us an average attendance that hovers under a hundred. While this is a big improvement, we seem to be at a plateau. One of our goals is to break the one hundred mark each week by next year. To do this we will need to get more lay people actively involved in different aspects of evangelism and improve our music by doing more with choirs in both services. We are also in the early stages of a plan to initiate a form of cell or shepherding groups within the congregation.

Matches have been found and the candles are lit. Our Spanish service is under way. It is undeniably more staid than the English. One reason is that the proportion of adults to children is reversed. In this service the tension between respect for the older group and mission with the new is more marked. When I arrived the Spanish group was using the liturgy from Liturgia Luterana (a translation of the *LBW* with different musical setting) and hymns from Culto Cristiano. We have continued using the liturgy since they had just become accustomed to it in the past few years. We make seasonal substitutions, however, with some new music in different sections. The hymns from Culto Cristiano are all old Protestant and Lutheran standbys translated into a rather antiquated Spanish. There are no Caribbean rhythms or melodies.

If I were beginning a new Spanish worship service, I doubt that we would use much if anything from Culto Cristiano. In our case, however, I have not felt it right to throw it out altogether. Over the years, this music has in fact become part of the spiritual life rhythms of our older members. It is this music that thrills their hearts and comforts them in times of suffering and loss. I make it a point to include two hymns from Culto Cristiano each week.

It is at Christmas time, however, that a rhythm besides those of Culto Cristiano begins to take hold of our older members as they remember the *aguinaldos* and *posadas* of their youth. *Aguinaldos*

are folkloric Christmas music of Puerto Rico. *Posadas* are pro-
cessions led by a couple representing Mary and Joseph. They go
visiting homes in search of *posada,* a resting place. As they walk,
they sing and receive treats to eat in the different homes.

One evening after an Advent Bible study, refreshments were
served and the group wanted to sing. Perhaps memories were stirred
by the fact that we were eating some of the very same delicious
treats served on warm Christmas nights. Soon someone began to
sing *aguinaldos* and others joined in. Helena, a member of the church
since its beginning days, went to an old chest in the corner, dusty
as the old baptismal font. She lifted the lid and pushed through
layers of old blankets until, from the very bottom, she lifted out an
oblong object wrapped in tissue paper. Slowly she unwrapped it—
a *guiro!* (Puerto Rican rhythm instrument). At that point, one of
the men noticed a set of *maracas* tied together and hanging on the
wall as a decoration. He took them from the wall, untied them, and
carried them into the kitchen to wash them off. What had been dug
up from beneath the layers, dusted, and washed off was their own
precious island heritage. What singing, laughter, and dancing followed! And what a joyous Christmas Eve we celebrated as the
transition from living room to sanctuary was finally made. Over the
next year I hope that we will be able to incorporate such music more
regularly into our worship life.

1:15 P.M. Vayen en Paz. Sirvan al Senor. "Go in Peace, Serve
the Lord." The Spanish service is over. It's the last Sunday of the
month and Ruben gives me my salary check made possible by the
national church. Half of our budget is synodical and national funding.
Although we are growing in numbers and stewardship, I see no end
to this situation. Still, I do not consider us to be a dependent congregation. Like all congregations, we are interdependent. We all
need each other. We do depend on others for some of the resources
we need to fulfill our ministry here, but others depend on us to be
here in mission and to bring our gifts and vision to bear on the life
of the whole church.

As an urban, multicultural congregation growing poorer as our
ministry grows richer, we have something to teach about being the
church, about the gospel and theology. There is certainly nothing

holy or romantic about being poor, but because the people of our neighborhood do not benefit from the basic idolatries of our society, which also affect our church, they have a vital, corrective vision to offer. If the ELCA is really serious about growing in our faithfulness to live out our identity as One, Holy, Catholic and Apostolic Church, they need us.

2:00 P.M. The church doors are locked, but continue to proclaim their brightly painted message of good news meant for all. As I walk home, my feelings are usually up or down depending on whether or not it was a "good" Sunday. At this point a "good" Sunday means 90-99 people (could we count Shavon, who is pregnant, for two and thus hit 100?), some new faces, no big fights, wonderful music. A "bad" Sunday means 75 people, the organist called at the last minute to say she couldn't come, no new faces, old ones missing, the acolytes were not being reverent, and the processional cross smashed into the font.

The mood change that I experience on Sunday mornings, depending upon what I perceive to be happening, the results of my labors so to speak, raises an issue that affects many urban churches. It is the idolatry of failure. While there is much to be said about our society's idolizing of success, I have found idolatry of failure to be a greater problem. It pervades the neighborhood. Why bother going to school, looking for a job, getting off drugs, if there seems to be no hope of a better life? Defeat and despair claim many lives that rightly belong to the living God. Add to that the feelings of long-time church members who have watched the deterioration not only of the neighborhood but of their congregation. It is tempting to feel that the glory days will never return, to be unhappy with anything that is tried because it will never be as it was. But thanks be to God who shows us again and again that ministry here is no dead end, that this truly is the place where God is at home and radiant glory is around the corner, soon and very soon, as the song says.

As I near the parsonage, I look forward to the lunch my husband has left out for me. By now he is probably upstairs taking a nap with Ana. I think about Ana. I remember one of the most wonderful moments of pregnancy was feeling her quickening movements begin inside me. Like John the Baptist, Ana's ministry began while she was still in the womb (perhaps I should count Shavon's unborn baby after all). Even on the worst days, the days when nothing seemed to go right, with nothing but dead bones around every corner and I was more aware of things falling apart than coming together, I would feel a kick in the gut, a poke in the ribs and I would be immediately cheered. It was Ana reminding me that new life was taking shape, growing and becoming stronger day by day. What a –wonderful image for the life of the spirit here! Even on grim days when the colors seem just painted on, new life is kicking up a storm. The Word has become flesh here at 156th Street and Prospect Avenue in the South Bronx, and we at Transfiguration behold grace upon grace. Thanks be to God! Gracias a Dios!

Note: the names of parish members have been changed.

CHAPTER **7**

One Congregation's Vision

James J. Lobdell

Holy Trinity Evangelical Lutheran Church is located in Inglewood, California. Although a separate city of 100,000 people, Inglewood is surrounded by Los Angeles and is considered part of the greater Los Angeles metropolitan area. Until 1965 the city was an exclusively white community in which persons of color were not welcome, as evidenced by a curfew law restricting any black person from entering the city after sunset. Within this environment, Holy Trinity, like the six other Lutheran churches in Inglewood, flourished. With its many programs for all ages and an attractive facility that included a fully equipped gymnasium, the church grew to a membership of over a thousand.

Everything changed, however, with the Watts riot in 1965. Watts is located three miles east of Inglewood, and apparently many families thought that was too close. The late 1960s and early 1970s saw rapid transitions in the city, as long-time residents sold their homes at bargain prices and provided the opportunity for black families to move into the community.

By the late 1970s membership had plummeted and worship attendance hovered between fifty to sixty persons. Because of dwindling resources, the church was forced to rent out its facilities just to survive. During this time a synodical study of Holy Trinity concluded that it would be best for the congregation to disband.

However, a small group persisted. A few long-time members were joined by a small number of newer community members who

78

were impressed by Holy Trinity's educational program and a worship that did not "last so long, beg for money, or have all that shouting and carrying on." This small group had a vision of what Holy Trinity could be, given proper leadership and commitment to the gospel. They knew, as the Scripture says: "Where there is no prophecy, the people cast off restraint" (Prov. 29:18). It was through their perseverance, toil, and patience that black families were gradually welcomed and the leadership of the church was transferred. Today all twelve deacons of the church council are black.

Over the last nine years, Holy Trinity's membership has increased to over 300 baptized persons (88 percent of whom are black) with an average worship attendance of 130. Today, the church's program includes: a Christian preschool, as well as a Head Start program; education that includes weekly Bible study, Sunday school, confirmation, first communion classes, acolyte classes, marriage seminars, money management workshops, and programs on health and diet; fellowship groups for seniors, adult men, adult women, young adults, junior youth and senior youth; an Interfaith Emergency Services program to assist families in need; and a weekly prayer and healing service. Holy Trinity has become a model congregation for the Evangelical Lutheran Church in America for ministry in a multicultural context. All of this happened because there were people at Holy Trinity with a vision.

A Vision for Worship

In my first weeks at Holy Trinity I was tempted to launch an aggressive evangelism effort. I knew from past experience, however, that such an effort would bring few, if any, results. Instead, I told the members, "Don't invite visitors to our church—not yet."

First we needed to have something to which we could invite people. Before making changes in any other area of Holy Trinity's ministry, it was essential that our worship life be expanded to include and involve people from our community, most of whom were black persons with Baptist, Methodist, or African-Methodist-Episcopal (AME) church backgrounds. This was no easy task for a Lutheran church whose traditional form and style of worship does not readily serve congregations in transition.

Although liturgy essentially means "the work of the people," more often than not Lutheran worship is not so much "the work of the *people*" as it is "the work of the *pastors.*" The people become spectators who watch rather than worship.

Sermons are typically more concerned with presenting theology than with touching the hearts and consciences of the people. In the same way, hymns that are difficult to sing are used because of their lyrics, whereas familiar old favorites are excluded because they present "bad" theology. Spontaneous expressions of feeling are generally considered out of place, because they break up the "reverence" of worship.

Finally, we Lutherans rely heavily on a book. Throughout the service, with our heads buried in the book, we are forever concerned about what page we are supposed to be on. It seems that we cannot sing, pray, respond, or say "amen" without a book! Consequently, for many Lutherans, Sunday morning has become primarily an intellectual exercise, and worship is more *cere*bration than *cele*bration.

This was brought home to me in a dramatic way by an elderly woman suffering with cancer. She was in her eighties and had been an active member of the Lutheran church all her life. She was terribly distressed. The doctor had told her that the cancer was inoperable and that radiation treatments would be necessary. During the visit, she asked, "Pastor, would you pray for me?" "Of course," I answered, but then I also encouraged her to pray for herself. She became very anxious at that point and said, "I don't know how—I don't know how to pray." Here was a woman who had attended church for over eighty years but in her hour of need was unable to utter a prayer. All those years of worship had not touched her enough to enable her to *feel* her faith and talk to God on her own.

At Holy Trinity, therefore, we have involved the whole person as well as the whole parish in worship. By whole *person* we mean not just one's mind and thinking but also one's spirit and soul, feelings and emotions, hopes and dreams—one's whole being. By whole *parish* we mean not only the members of our congregation but also people in the surrounding community. Thus our liturgy, rather than being imposed on the people, arises from the people and reflects the black community in which we serve. The people we invite to church participate and are truly involved in the worship celebration, because the liturgy is "their own work."

We have also expanded our hymnody. I shall never forget the woman who lived down the block from the church. Each week she would see me and ask, "Pastor, what are the hymns for Sunday?" Assuming that she must love to sing our hymns, I would always give a complete listing. And each time she would then ask, "And what are the numbers of those hymns?" to which I responded with the numbers as well. But I always thought it peculiar that during Sunday worship the woman never sang. Then one day she came rushing into the church, shouting, "Pastor, I hit it—255! I hit the number!" Lo and behold, she had been "playing the numbers" (gambling) with the hymns each week! Other than that, the hymns meant nothing to her. They were, as she said, not very familiar. Obviously for this woman, and others like her, we needed to expand our repertoire of hymns.

How do Lutheran churches experiencing transition expand their hymnody? It is true that there are good old Protestant hymns, like "All Hail the Power of Jesus' Name" and "The Church's One Foundation," which are powerful and moving. But there are also hymns like "Blessed Assurance" and "Leaning on the Everlasting Arms," which are sometimes criticized for their "bad" theology but which are universally known and loved by the people.

Hymns that reflect the particular community the church is serving should be included as well. In our predominantly black community, we also sing gospel music, new and old, and spirituals. At Holy Trinity, we searched for a long time before finding just the right accompanist who, be it in a Bach chorale or black spiritual, allows people to sing from the soul.

We also encourage people to respond as they feel in worship. Then feelings and emotions, as well as thoughts and ideas, are expressed. Responses like "amen" and clapping are encouraged. Greeting and welcoming others is also part of the service. This openness to the Spirit encourages spontaneity.

This expression of feelings begins with the presiding minister. In worship that is celebration the pastor must be free to share emotions and feelings as well as thoughts and ideas, so that the people are convinced that the good news of Jesus Christ is something that affects the pastor at the deepest level. Preachers at Holy Trinity do not read their sermons. Rather, they preach them with conviction and feeling. Sometimes the preacher literally comes down from the pulpit to where the people are to preach. Rather than reading from a book, the presiding minister leads parts of worship using his or her own words, even initiating dialogue with the people, so that they are called upon to respond and contribute to the worship experience.

Finally, for the people to feel involved, it is important that their needs and concerns be taken seriously. One way to hear people's needs and concerns is to have a time in the worship service for sharing of those concerns; this sharing is done not only by the presiding minister but by anyone who is present. This is not just an "announcement time" but an integral part of worship, because the concerns are then prayed for in the service. As the presiding minister encourages the offering of petitions, lay liturgists as well as church council members are challenged to lead the congregation in prayer. Background music from the organ or piano helps set a prayerful mood and encourages individual petitions.

Once we had incorporated these strategies in our worship at Holy Trinity, we were ready to invite visitors.

A Vision for Witness

For successful evangelism in the city, most urban pastors are trained to be aggressive and highly visible in the local community. Such an approach involves systematic door-to-door calling on families, periodic walks through the neighborhood to keep in touch with what's happening in the community, and immediate contact with new arrivals to invite them to the church.

These efforts may work well in cities like New York and Philadelphia, where the streets are alive with activity during the day and where there exists a strong sense of neighborhood. In the urban sprawl of Los Angeles, however, people are not as connected with a particular community and spend much of their time on freeways, so such efforts are often in vain. In our community a pastor could walk for blocks before meeting another person in the neighborhood of our church and may knock on twenty doors before finding anyone home.

Consequently, the evangelistic approach we have found to be most effective is one of "visit us before we visit you." This approach seeks to make the initial contact with individuals and families at our Sunday worship rather than within the home. We are confident that after experiencing our worship and fellowship on Sunday morning, families will later be receptive and interested in our visits.

We have found that the best way for us to identify potential members has been through the invitations of current members and friends. Here again our worship service is the key. If our members and friends feel involved and inspired on Sunday morning, then they will want to invite others to share their experience. Since the challenge, then, is to get people to attend our worship that first time, at Holy Trinity we provide ample opportunities for inviting guests. Every quarter we have a Visitor's Sunday to encourage members to invite family, friends, coworkers, and others—"each one bring one," and after worship we enjoy fellowship with our guests over a delicious potluck luncheon in the parish hall. There are Children's Sundays, and special occasions that provide opportunities for members to involve their extended families. We rarely have a Sunday without visitors.

For such evangelistic efforts to be effective, however, witness must be integral to worship. At Holy Trinity, we take time during worship to introduce our visitors and make them feel welcome. Thus members know who is visiting and are encouraged to get acquainted at the fellowship hour afterward. Subsequently, each visitor is called by the pastor, with aggressive follow-up if desired. Most of our new members have come this way.

We also take seriously our evangelistic role to introduce or reacquaint people with the Word of God. There are Bibles in every pew and all Scripture lessons are read together from the Bible. Each Sunday's sermon centers around a Scripture text, which also provides the theme for that day. During the sermon the congregation is encouraged to dialogue with the preacher and, using their Bibles, the pastor and the people, together, "break open" the text. In this way, both minister and the congregation are constantly being challenged by the Word.

Worship and witness are also connected by the affirmation of faith, which in the LBW liturgy is the reciting of the Creed in response to the sermon.

At Holy Trinity we have expanded the affirmation of faith to include the opportunity for those persons who have felt especially touched or challenged during worship to stand or come forward. A verse from a familiar hymn is sung to support them. The whole congregation then joins them in reciting the Creed and affirming that "I believe." Last Thanksgiving over twenty people came to the altar; on Mother's Day several mothers and children came forward together; some Sundays no one feels so moved. But on each Sunday we do provide the opportunity to respond and affirm, as the gospel song says:

> He touched me, O He touched me,
> And O the joy that floods my soul;
> Something happened, and now I know,
> He touched me and made me whole.

A Vision for Learning

Most of us were educated by a system that sought to impart information from the teacher to the student. Education consisted largely of filling empty heads with knowledge. The interest was in teaching people *what* to think rather than *how* to think. But how can we seek out the gifts of people from different backgrounds if only the teacher has something to offer?

If we are to respect and appreciate the different backgrounds, experiences, and cultures represented in a multicultural setting, then we as teachers must use a method of education that seeks to teach *how* to think rather than *what* to think. Such a method does not say, "Let me tell you what this means," but rather asks, "What do you think it means?" Taking seriously what the student brings to the learning situation encourages a cooperative effort in discovery of the truth.

Incorporating this method at Holy Trinity, we have discovered that Bible study can be more a time of transformation than information. Parishioners can discover for themselves what is true. Rather than merely conforming to religious or social norms, they discern for themselves what God wants them to be and do in their daily lives.

In addition, educational programs at Holy Trinity reflect our multicultural setting. The commemoration of Dr. Martin Luther King's birthday has become as significant as Reformation Sunday; Black History Month has a special place in the church year; the African celebration of Kwanzaa is recognized along with Christmas; the Maundy Thursday passover service emphasizes the themes of freedom and justice; and the church paraments, banners, and symbols reflect the colors and cultures of our members.

A Vision of Support

Another problem for congregations experiencing transition is that many members who have joined in recent years do not really feel that the church belongs to them. They do not have the historical perspective or the long-standing ties of church members in more stable situations.

Consequently, their perspective may be like that expressed in one of my favorite stories about a struggling congregation. When their pastor preached that if their church was going to grow and become stronger it would have to *crawl* first, the people responded: "Let it crawl, pastor." "Then after this church crawls, it must *stand,*" said the pastor. "Let it stand," replied the people. Encouraged by their enthusiasm, the pastor continued, "Then after this church stands, it must *walk.*" "Let it walk, pastor," came the response. "And then this church must *run!*" "Let it run, pastor!" they exclaimed. Finally, all excited, the pastor shouted, "And if this church is going to run, its members must *give!*" And the members cried out, "Let it crawl, pastor, *please* let it crawl!" To challenge such an attitude, it is important for members to take ownership of their church.

Ownership begins with taking control of the church property. During the time of transition, as resources dwindle, congregations often "rent out" their space to community groups. This encourages good community relations and provides additional support for the church budget. It can also convey the message—both to the members and to the community—that this is somebody else's church.

When I came to Holy Trinity, a Seventh Day Adventist congregation worshiped there on Saturday, used the church on Tuesdays and Thursdays for special programs, and was requesting more time and space for additional activities. Slowly it was becoming unclear to the community what kind of church *we* were and what kind of programs *we* offered. Did we worship on Saturday or Sunday? It was not until the Seventh Day Adventist congregation went elsewhere and we initiated new programs of our own that it became clear whose church this was.

In addition, repairs and refurbishment were badly needed. So special projects were undertaken to upgrade the building. Some projects were done by members; others, like painting the exterior and interior of the church, required fund-raising and special expertise. As members invested themselves in improving the church property, a change occurred. It is amazing what a newly painted church can do for the self-image of a congregation. Suddenly, people were talking about how nice our church looked and how we needed to take better care of it!

That leads me to a point about stewardship. One of the temptations of pastors serving transitional congregations is to treat the people as "deprived." While it is true that often there may be economic and numerical limitations, treating people as deprived is patronizing and becomes more harmful than helpful. People who are treated as deprived tend to act deprived.

On the contrary, in times of transition, people need to be challenged to take responsibility and pledge themselves to supporting the ministry of their church. They may say, "Well, I can't pledge" or "I don't pledge." But is that true? They pledge when they use a Master Card. The question is not whether they pledge but to what they pledge.

At Holy Trinity we encourage all of our members to make an annual commitment toward the ministry of our church. Each pledge includes not only a financial commitment but a listing of the talents and interests of the person, and an indication of the areas within the church in which he or she would like to serve. In this way we have taken ownership and made it clear that our church is ready to stand, to walk, and even run—our church is not going to "crawl" anymore!

A Vision of Service

"If I can help somebody as I pass along," proclaims a gospel hymn, "then my living will not be vain." The transition of a congregation is not complete until that congregation moves beyond its own concerns for survival and growth to a concern for the whole community and the welfare of its neighbors.

Consider the story about the young woman who went with her grandmother to a highly emotional worship service in which people were clapping, shouting, and even jumping about. She asked her grandmother if all the jumping and shouting meant that people were really being touched by the Holy Spirit, or whether it was just some kind of emotional release. Her grandmother thought for a moment and then replied, "It's not how high they jump that counts. It's what they do when they come down that tells you if it's the real thing!"

The present challenge at Holy Trinity is to help and empower members to live a Christian life after "coming down" from worship. We are fed and nurtured by the gospel on Sunday mornings, but how might we serve in Gospel-directed ways through the week? How might the gospel be applied to our relationships and life situations? And how might we as a church better serve our community?

In response to this challenge, we are moving from an emphasis on helping the *church* function better to helping *people* function better. For example, during Lent we offer professionally led seminars designed to strengthen various aspects of members' lives. In addition, we have entered into an ecumenical arrangement with ten other churches in the Inglewood community to provide Interfaith Emergency Services. Staffed by a Lutheran Social Services coordinator, this program gives emergency assistance and advocacy for those in need. We hope to move beyond providing temporary relief toward promoting changes at a long-term level in our community.

As a white pastor serving in a predominantly black community, I often hear well-meaning people suggest that I really do not belong where I am. As I think back on my years as a pastor, most of my ministry has been in situations where supposedly I did not belong.

I always recall, however, the Sunday morning many years ago in the Harlem church where I had been assigned for internship. I was wondering "What on earth am I doing here?" I was feeling especially lonely and discouraged, when a woman from the choir rose to sing:

> I sing because I'm happy,
> I sing because I'm free,
> For His eye is on the sparrow,
> And I know He watches me.

At that moment I realized that she and I had something in common that was more powerful than any of our differences. We shared a faith in the Lord Jesus Christ, a faith that had the power to bring us together and enabled us to rise above the walls of race and culture to affirm our unity in Christ. At that moment I realized on more than just an intellectual level, that: "There is no longer Jew or Greek, there is no longer slave or free, there is no longer male and female; for all of you are one in Christ Jesus" (Gal. 3:28). This powerful truth can sustain and encourage people working together in urban ministries like that of Holy Trinity in Inglewood, California. We are not as different from one another as we might think!

CHAPTER **8**

New Life for Church and Community

Mary and David T. Nelson

We arrived on Chicago's West Side on a hot August evening in 1965. Three days later, we were coming home after a concert, and just as we got off the expressway near the house, some folks yelled to us, "shut your car, shut your car." We barely got the top of our Volkswagen closed when rocks, bricks, and bottles were showered on the car. That was the beginning of the riot that wracked our community, a sign of the anguish and despair of a poor, black community that saw little hope. The riot started because a young mother standing at a street corner had been struck and killed by a careening fire truck. The community had been picketing the fire station for months to get black firemen on the staff.

It wasn't always like that. Bethel Lutheran Church, begun in 1890 by immigrants in a working-class community on Chicago's West Side, grew until it had an active congregation of over 500 members. Between 1960 and 1965, 35,000 white people moved out and 60,000 black people moved into our square-mile area and the church began dwindling. When I was called to serve there in 1965, just thirty-five active elderly white members were left. I was fortunate to have been called by a bishop who mandated me to help that church learn how to serve its community. In my previous ministry, I had started a new mission church in the suburbs, where there were proven methods for gathering a congregation.

But on Chicago's West Side, the riot changed the dynamics of mission. Instead of calling on people one by one, welcoming them to church, and beginning a congregation in that way, suddenly the fires were all around us. What strength remained in this little band of people had to be used to deal with hurt so great that it caused a riot. That very moment, which seemed like the threat of death itself, brought the power of God's resurrection into our midst in ways we could see. The gospel says that those who lose life for the sake of the gospel will find it, and that was true for us.

While maintaining loving service to the elderly white people who had stayed faithful to the church, much time and effort were also used to work with other pastors and churches in the community. Together we asked the people, "What caused the riot? What brought us to destroy our own community?" After thinking through this with many people, we discovered that the number one problem was the loss of hope. Parents said, "When we see our kids getting less education than we got down south, when we see our children with less than we had before, that causes despair, that causes anger, that causes a riot!"

We started meeting with other pastors in the community to look for a response. Combining our efforts and guided by the needs expressed, we started by sponsoring an after school tutoring program. We pooled our resources and reached out to suburban churches to augment our own tutors. We gathered the kids from the schools around the churches, and started on a shoestring budget. As a result, the kids got used to coming into the church, and it wasn't so hard to say, "Why don't you come to Sunday school?" Since the kids had gotten to feel at home there, they started to come to an all-white church and Sunday school. It was natural, then, to reach behind them to their parents and invite them. They now knew the church cared. They could hear from their own kids the gift of love that had been shared. Just two months after the tutoring program had begun, the first black members joined Bethel.

As the churches continued in this cooperative effort, we soon became aware of how big the task was, how great the needs were, and how limited our resources were. This pushed us together—it was too much for any one of us. We sought and received about $10,000 in denominational funding to hire two staff members and start a combined program. Much to our joy, it began to blossom. More and more kids came into each church, and then we started considering other programs. We soon established a day-care center, an employment center and other projects.

Cooperative ministry, however, has its limitations. Our common effort grew large and "successful," but also became diverted from the gospel core of serving others. Bethel had to return to its own church base after thirteen years, to stay true to that gospel mandate. We continued our programs, moved in new directions, and now participate in networks focused around particular issues or programs.

Bethel church grew by meeting people through these programs. Always the invitation was to come to church on Sunday for that is the source of abiding strength. People who saw the church at work responded; this was the kind of church where they wanted to belong. We became a meeting place, a place for funerals of community activists; all of these contacts with Bethel and its people drew others in. It didn't happen quickly. For almost two years we asked people to sit up front so it wouldn't seem so empty. It took time to get a choir together, but as our choir evolved, we soon found that it needed to be a gospel choir to express the community experience.

By this time our community was 95 percent black. About one-third of the families were on welfare or received some kind of assistance. We had an unemployment rate of 19 percent and the neighborhood was neglected by the city.

Some years later, responding to the expressed needs of the parents, we started a Christian grade school. Thirty-five families put up $100 each; that was the seed fund that got it all started. There was no difference in tuition between members and nonmembers, but we did ask parents to belong to a Christian church. After a few years some parents became a part of our church family, finding it a place of hope and value. Now the church and the school serve each other, and about 35 percent of the parents belong to church.

Other programs have had the same effect. By 1979 our community was losing two hundred units of housing a year. If we didn't do something about the housing, there wouldn't be a community left. The congregation voted to start a housing ministry and once again sought to put together $5,000 to do this. To finance such projects, we have had to mortgage the church building a number of times, but we have always been able to pay it back. We also had help from the denomination in the form of borrowing authority. Thus Bethel New Life, Inc., a separate but related corporation, was formed. Its executive director is Mary Nelson, who came to Bethel after missionary service in Africa. We started with three flats, purchased for $275 and needing total rehabilitation.

Over the years, the congregation's involvement in the housing ministry has taken different forms. The congregation, all community people themselves, has been cosigner on notes, has given mortgages for projects, has acted as "sponsor," has given demand promissory notes. Some "sweat equity" projects have called for many work days, and congregation members have faithfully turned out each time to work and work on a building so others could have decent, affordable housing. People helping others with no apparent self-interest has been a strong witness to the community.

Sunday morning worship announcement time has called for people to go down to city hall to demonstrate, or show support for a project, or push a reluctant city or county agency into action, and the Bethel bus has made many such treks. In desperate times, calls were made to the prayer circle, and many folks went down on their knees to give hope for overcoming one of the many obstacles blocking a desperately needed project. Sunday morning worship prayer time often includes the most current project and the problems it faces. When we finally do get a project completed, we always dedicate it on Sundays, starting with the celebration of morning worship, marching down the street (all our projects are within four blocks of the church) with balloons and choirs and pastors and people and singing gospel songs. Recently, when we dedicated the Living-Learning Center, a school that now provides both housing and educational space, we declared it a miracle and used the theme, "With humanity it is impossible, but with God, all things are possible." The newspapers used that verse of Scripture in their headlines.

Some of our programs will never be a significant source of new members for the church. This is true of our wholistic health center, which concentrates on the urgent medical, social and spiritual needs of our community, on the infant mortality problem, and on broken families. The medical and counseling resources are strained to the limit, and we have a continuing need for funds to keep going.

These programs demonstrate that the church cares and provides life and hope. We believe it is a sign of God's grace that five of our young people, against all the odds, have become doctors, and that currently nine of our young people are in Lutheran colleges. Prospects for the next generation are even more promising since we have fifty young people in seventh and eighth grade confirmation.

Bethel Lutheran Church has become a central part of the community. Residents often call it "that Lutheran Baptist Church," for we combine the culture of the community with the Lutheran heritage. Sunday services are often two hours long and regularly include altar calls. Music is provided by a combined choir of over a hundred persons, both pipe and Hammond organs; the *Lutheran Book of Worship (LBW)* and gospel music are used. Sunday morning announcements include a great variety of concerns and interests.

Bethel congregation has grown to almost six hundred and the average weekly pledge is $17.50. We are now close to being a self-supporting congregation, despite early expectations that we would always need aid. The budget of the church is now over $100,000; from this has developed a nearly $3 million annual operating budget for community projects, employing about two hundred people. All this comes from a congregation of people with limited resources. God has really taken our five loaves and two fishes and multiplied them to feed the many. The church staff, however, has remained bare bones. There is only one full-time pastor, no secretary, no paid assistants. The rest of the staff are a part-time music director, a part-time organist, and a part-time custodian. There is a worker-pastor (volunteer) from the community. While this lean staffing has made room for a lot of people to help, it also means that the pastor is often youth leader, bus driver, and back-up custodian.

Pastoral ministry in this setting includes hospital visitation, crisis intervention, court appearances, and dealing with the destructive effects of poverty, racism, and violence. Pastoral ministry to individuals, community programs, and advocacy on issues are needed. It takes a variety of people to form this kind of ministry team.

What have we learned from these twenty years of urban ministry? (1) Don't wait until you are "strong" to start doing things; take a plunge into action, act with boldness (but not everyone needs riots to start this!). (2) We have to be willing to risk—whether it is to mortgage the church, or risk our time on putting things together that seem impossible. (3) Keep at the very center the gospel (the hope that is beyond hope); foster a praying core of people and the community of the faithful on Sunday. (4) Sacrificial giving starts with the leaders; that spirit is catching, and is critical to success. Bethel has always kept its benevolence commitments to the worldwide church, knowing that even though we may be poor in America, we are rich in the eyes of the world. In sharing we live. When people come to the church to get physical things, they leave poor. When people come ready to share from their hearts, they gather strength from the body of Christ. (5) The Lutheran heritage is enriched as it is blended with the culture of the community, and is combined creatively in the Sunday morning services.

In all that we do, we take as our statement of purpose that passage from Isaiah (58:9-12), which also accords with our experience:

> If you remove the yoke from among you, the pointing of the finger, the speaking of evil, if you offer your food to the hungry and satisfy the needs of the afflicted, then your light shall rise in the darkness and your gloom be like the noonday. The Lord will guide you continually, and satisfy your needs in parched places, and make your bones strong; and you shall be like a watered garden, like a spring of water, whose waters never fail. Your ancient ruins shall be rebuilt; you shall raise up the foundations of many generations; you shall be called the repairer of the breach, the restorer of streets to live in.

CHAPTER 9

Rebuilding the City

Edward A. Ruen

The practice of urban ministry in the Lutheran church has one goal and that is the rebuilding of our cities. Such a vision, audacious as it may seem, is consistent with what God expects from us as stewards.

When I first began my ministry in the late sixties and early seventies in the South Bronx, it was a time of great expectations arising out of the civil rights movement and the war on poverty. Most urban ministers during this period had visions of radical change in urban ghettos across the country: justice would come to the poor.

Like many urban parishes, our parish, St. Peter's, was deeply involved in new housing construction, advocacy related to state and city housing legislation, and block organizing of tenants. We had a parochial school and a residential treatment center for drug addicts. We had a special ministry to the large gangs roaming the streets. You name it, we had it—we were on a roll! The motto of the Brooklyn Black Panthers—"Roll on over or we will roll on over you" fit our urban ministry and the attitude of many of the poor.

I recall a Methodist church in East Harlem being liberated for the people of the community by the Young Lords. The congregation at the time, mostly white, was not meeting the needs of the community and consequently it needed to be liberated. The Young Lords moved in and took it over. One had to pass by armed guards to get into the church. The sanctuary had been turned into a health clinic and community center. There was the sound and smell of life in it.

In the midst of this sanctuary for the white middle class, which had become sanctuary for the minority poor, we held our daily worship. In those days "Power to the people" had a meaning and reality that it has lost today. The tide began to change with a new administration in Washington. It became clear that change wasn't happening as quickly as anticipated. One of our community organizations, "Better Housing for All," wanted to rehabilitate several tenements. I remember well the man from Housing and Urban Development (HUD), in Washington, who came to our meeting and told us that Nixon was going to freeze all funds for housing. Washington was no longer the friend of the poor or the city—times, they were a changing! On the community level, leadership was reduced because many of the best minority community leaders had been bought off by the various public programs. They took jobs that paid well but were, for the most part, a meaningless waste of community leadership. Community organizing wasn't as successful now that government and industry had pulled back as providers. It was nearly impossible to motivate the people and, often, the organizers themselves.

At the same time the local clergy of all denominations were getting worn down by the endless activity and lack of success. We pulled back, and because most of the clergy were middle class and white they would either leave or focus on congregational activities like worship and education. I took a year of study at Norwich State Hospital to rest up and pull out. I regret that I couldn't pace myself more while at St. Peter's; maybe if I had, we would still be there. All I know is that we lived and ministered as best we could in one of the most exhilarating and painful periods for the urban church in this century. So where do you go from there? After Norwich, I joined a pastoral team at Our Savior's Lutheran Church in downtown Milwaukee for five years. For the last eight years I have served as executive director of a community-based organization in Milwaukee called the Next Door Foundation.

Next Door began back in 1969 as a community-based youth ministry of Our Savior's Lutheran Church. It became a separate nonprofit corporation in 1972. Today the Foundation has thirty-six full-time and seventeen part-time staff, and serves over 3,600 individuals a year. Its programs include an outpatient drug and alcohol center, an alternative high school, an urban program for college students, a youth employment program, a tutoring program for six-through eleven-year-olds, a recreation program for children and youth, and a parenting program for parents with children from birth to five years old. In addition, the Foundation owns and manages three buildings which have a total of fifty-five apartments and commercial space. Over 77 percent of the people served are youth, 84 percent are minority.

The target area has seventy thousand people and covers one-tenth of Milwaukee. In April of 1986 we completed an analysis of the area with the following results:

Next Door Foundation target area experienced a greater population decline—19.1 percent in total population over the fifteen-year period—than the city of Milwaukee. Blacks now constitute the majority population in the target area. By 1980, the percentage of people in poverty within the target area was nearly three times that of the city of Milwaukee. Female-headed households, which earn only 38.15 percent of the income earned by two-parent families, constituted more than half of our target area families.

Our target area has a higher high school drop-out rate, more severe unemployment (particularly among youths), and a higher rate of infant mortality, teenage pregnancy, and drug use than one would find in many other neighborhoods. Yet our target area has much in common with cities across the nation. We are seeing the ever-widening gap between rich and poor with an impoverished, unemployed, illiterate underclass rapidly increasing in size. We see it in Milwaukee, Chicago, New York, and Los Angeles.

In my opening statement I said that the goal for urban ministry in the Lutheran church must be the rebuilding of the city. My first concern is that we have lost touch with the pain of poverty through the intellectualization of the problem and the Band-Aid approach of free meals, overnight shelter, and secondhand clothes. The pain of poverty can't be reduced through the charity of a few or the prayers of the many.

We stand at a crossroads as a church. One road leads to a continuation of the status quo: doing good in an effort to reduce our guilt as much as to satisfy the hungry. How often we hear a person say that "I got more back from giving than I gave." Seldom do I hear people cry or weep or scream because of the injustice of it all. We move like machines, in and out of the world of the poor, working at a distance sufficient to keep us from experiencing their pain.

The new road, however, begins with pain, outrage, and confession; it takes us into the homes of the despairing and the hungry. We cry ourselves to sleep because of the pain we feel from the bruises of the day. We drug ourselves in the morning to help us cope with dead-end lives. We die young. A Next Door is good but it isn't enough, a hot meal is good but it isn't enough, a night at the shelter is good but it isn't enough. The pain of urban poverty permeates all and impels me to confess and pray. I am convinced that there will never be an effective urban ministry by the Lutheran church unless there is a clear call that comes out of the pain and despair of the poor and is heard by a church that deeply feels with them. The first question for the Lutheran church—a white middle-class church—is whether we are willing to claim a comradeship with our brothers and sisters that is deep enough to cause us to suffer with them.

If the call to comradeship with the poor comes first in urban ministry, then the next priority is a healthy spiritual life. We face a crisis in our faith identity in the Lutheran church today that is a direct result of our having abandoned a disciplined life of prayer and Bible study. Ask clergy and laity how much time they spend at any one of those disciplines and you will discover how weak our discipline has become. As I said, the new road is not easy to take, it requires the very best spiritual conditioning for all who would take it. As I look back on those early days in the South Bronx I sometimes reflect on the fact that we had trusted not in God but in our own abilities. We were going to rebuild the city with or without God. But God was for the poor in our city long before we were, and God will be there long after we are gone. Are we as Lutherans spiritually conditioned for the challenges of urban ministry in the future? That is my second question.

Let us assume that we have that comradeship with the poor and that we are spiritually readied for the practice of urban ministry. What comes after that? What have we learned from the past that could assist us as we develop a strategy for the future?

We need a model. For me the time-tested model is Nehemiah, who responded to those in suffering and to God. This includes a programmatic approach for a decayed and demoralized urban community. Nehemiah challenges me to return to the city; Nehemiah scts before me and the church the vision of a rebuilt city, a city that will be rebuilt by the people of the city. If we have learned anything from the past it is that we cannot do the job by ourselves. We need to cooperate within the Lutheran church and beyond it if we are to accomplish anything.

Even more important, we need an urban strategy that will have as its goal the rebuilt city. What Nehemiah teaches is the need to assess, to plan, and finally to execute. The past has been filled with solo attempts at education, housing, or employment, but seldom has there been an overall plan to guide these activities. I know that is true in Milwaukee. We will not make the best use of our resources until such a defined and coordinated approach is adopted. It can't be adopted if we are talking about rebuilding half the city; it can only happen when the whole is taken into consideration. Maybe we cannot do this in all cities at once, but we can develop approaches in several cities that will be models for others. The example of Nehemiah teaches us that we need everyone if we are to build this new city. Should our goal be maintaining our theology, or our religious status quo, or a meal program, then we don't need everyone. If it is the rebuilding of the city, we need everyone: rich and poor, Jew and Orthodox, Republican and Democrat, young and old, literate and illiterate, and the private and public sectors. Nehemiah asks the Lutheran church to have faith in God and a plan for rebuilding the city.

PART THREE

Emboldened by Hope:
the Future of Lutheran Mission and Ministry
in Changing Urban Communities

CHAPTER 10

The Clown: An Image of Hope from the Church in the City

Margaret Wold

Once, while I was returning from a meeting in another city, I was assigned a seat on the airplane next to a friendly and loquacious rodeo cowboy. After learning that he had once suffered a fall that broke his neck and lower back and later another fall which broke four ribs and punctured his lung, I made the wholly inadequate observation that his profession was risky business.

"Yes, ma'am," he drawled, "There's risk involved for the rider in the rodeo, but the dangers for us aren't anywhere near as great as the ones the rodeo clowns take. They're the ones we owe our lives to."

"What do rodeo clowns do that's so dangerous?" I asked.

He told me about this special breed of clowns who reserve their funniest routines for that most dangerous of all rodeo events, riding the bulls. Their comic antics distract the twisting, stomping, goring animal away from the thrown cowboy. They deliberately wear bright clothing to attract the bull's attention and roll around in wooden barrels that tempt him to drive his horns into them. The audience, unaware of the real purpose of the comic business going on in the arena, laughs in relief as potential tragedy for the thrown cowboy is translated by the clowns into hilarious comedy.

While the most obvious analogy we can make out of the rodeo clown is that of a savior, a "Christ-figure," it's not that particular aspect of the role that caught my attention. All of my unfocused thoughts about clowns, comedies, and cities took coherent shape around the clown who enters into a tragic situation, turns it inside out, and forces us to see that there are other options, comic and hopeful, in the midst of the tragic.

The tragedy of the city is that it promises so much and delivers so little. It promises freedom, freedom from the unrelenting sunup to sundown toil that has plagued farmers and herdsmen from the dawn of history. Streetlights promise release from primitive terrors of the dark. A trip to the market offers the fruits of the fields without any of the backbreaking labor that went into their production. The steaks and chops that lie in orderly rows in meat cases give no hint of the anxieties that tormented their growers. To city dwellers bad weather is simply an inconvenience, not a matter of survival.

Entertainment events are offered twenty-four-hours-a-day, seven days a week. Spas, racquetball courts, bowling alleys, dance halls, and jazzercise classes promise everlasting health and vitality. Life is an endless highway on which one can cruise as long as fuel lasts. No one needs to think, to feel, to stoop, or to confront the emptiness and the silence inside of one's self.

The promise seduces; but the reality kills. The income needed to participate in the glittering parade eludes most people's grasp. Society's racist structures deny opportunity to all but the most ambitious and gifted people of color, and both young and old alike find drugs and alcohol a way of escape from the squalor of the streets and the emptiness of existence. Youngsters who have left their homes to seek love, fame, and fortune in the city find instead exploitation, prostitution, and entrapment when they get there.

After generations of the church's presence in the city, the homeless still sleep on sidewalk heating grates and in the doorways of buildings at night; the jobless still lie on park benches or stand on the street corners in the daytime. Trash, litter, and graffiti continue to disfigure the concrete and asphalt. Muggings, knifings, and shootings still terrorize the inhabitants and the sirens of emergency vehicles persist in screaming their shrill counterpoint to the throbbing bass of traffic noises.

The props never seem to change. The stage is always set for tragedy. Factories with cold chimneys and silent assembly lines refuse to hear the cries of the jobless on the streets around them, their owners long gone to faraway lands, having been lured there by cheaper labor markets and larger profits. Boarded-up churches bear mute testimony to members and pastors who moved to the comparative safety of the suburbs. Even the urban Catholic parish has been shrinking steadily, says a report by the Notre Dame Study of Catholic Parish Life. "The suburban parish," the authors tell us, "is replacing the urban neighborhood parish as the normative experience for a plurality of Catholics."[1]

It's time then to send in the clowns! The rodeo rider is down and the bull twists and stomps with excitement at the bloody prospect of pushing his horns through the enemy he's spilled from his back. In the stands, the spectators hide their faces, peeking through their fingers at the horror that is coming.

Let's send in the clowns! Divert the crowds, distract the bull, turn the imminent tragedy into comedy. "We have become a spectacle to the world. . . . We are fools for the sake of Christ . . ." (1 Cor. 4:9-10) said Paul as he went from one city to another to announce the crazy and gracious good news that one of the men their soldiers had crucified had risen from the dead.

Yet what in the world can a pastor do to make any difference in the tragic realities of the city? Will being there make any difference in the crime rates? Can the church keep even one factory from closing and moving overseas to a cheaper labor market? Do the churches near the skid rows and sunset strips of our cities make any difference to the pimps and pushers who work those avenues?

Into the urban arenas come the clowns in their clergy collars, black suits, and pectoral crosses peddling their good news, and preaching, as Frederick Buechner says, "the king who looks like a tramp, the prince of peace who looks like the prince of fools, the lamb of God who ends like something hung up at the butcher's."[2]

In the late sixties and early seventies when all hell was breaking loose in the cities of our country, and when most urban pastors were stereotyped as growing scraggly hair and beards, wearing faded blue jeans, and playing protest songs on their guitars, a little, old-fashioned, square, straight, almost ready-to-retire pastor was called to a restless, exploding city church that had declined suddenly from a membership of eighteen hundred to four hundred persons when everybody with white skin decided to move away from their darker-skinned neighbors.

This small, Charlie Chaplin-like man began to walk up and down the hostile, gang-ridden streets of his neighborhood, knocking on doors, handing out his calling card, and telling people that he was the new Lutheran pastor from that church over there on the corner and to call on him if they ever needed a friend. The house he and his white haired wife lived in was right across the street from the church building. It was burglarized five times that first year and twice vandals set fires in the middle of their living room. So they put bars on the windows and locks on the doors, but they stayed. They planted flowers in the church yard and the pastor's wife gave piano lessons to the children in the summertime and they stayed ten years.

When the pastor and his wife left, the membership was half black and half white and for an hour every Sunday after church they all stayed together drinking coffee and treating each other to goodies and hugs in one of the most loving Christian communities they had ever been in. The pastor-clown had brought another reality into that church and neighborhood. He believed that what he was doing was making a difference and he kept on doing what he believed in.

There are pastors who playact at ministry in the city, pastors who don't "believe that the problem is real," and as a result aren't committed to what they are doing. Their routines are borrowed and they are little involved with them. Since most denominations have minimal or no expectations that anything is going to happen in the city, some pastors find urban parishes a cozy place to hide, just getting by, going through the motions, drinking beer with their cronies and enjoying feeling neglected by the synod office.

One Sunday morning I visited a congregation where thirty-five elderly white people were in the pews. Now thirty-five is a large number of disciples if you consider what the original twelve-minus-one-plus-one were able to accomplish. So I'm not ridiculing the size of any worshiping group. The tragedy here was that they were uninvolved with the material they were given to work with. That material was a community overwhelmingly composed of Spanish-speaking people who lived in large, extended families in the tract homes surrounding the church. In the playground of the nearby elementary school, Mexican-American children chattered in both English and Spanish.

But inside that sanctuary of a Sunday morning, the pastor carried on his business as though the other reality did not exist. Since I was the guest preacher, I was asked to march in with the choir of ten members, the pastor and two acolytes. The pastor's most pressing concern that morning was that the ten members of the choir march in with precisely the same amount of space between them. They were to allow exactly four steps by the two members in front of them before they started down the aisle. I was also carefully instructed as to which side of the chancel I was to sit in and how long I was to remain "reverencing" the altar before I moved to that side.

I knew that what we were so seriously engaged in inside that sanctuary had no relationship at all to what I knew about that neighborhood. What we were doing left untouched the tragic realities affecting so many lives—the high rate of unemployment in those homes, the high state of anxiety caused by constant Immigration and Naturalization Service sweeps and the high drop-out rate of secondary school students as they faced a seemingly hopeless future. We were playing out a comic fantasy, about as effective in speaking a word of hope to that community as a pratfall or a pie in the face.

By structuring our small universe with problems we can control, like how many steps are correct in a processional, we can pretend that there is no world out there which faces us at every turn with insoluble problems and complex dilemmas. "Just enter into our fantasy with us," we invite, "and all of your real problems will vanish. Poverty, famine, unemployment, violence, all of them will not exist for you any more."

To be a bringer of hope the clown must have entered into the agony of the city and discovered laughter and hope in the heart of tragedy. This is not a call to triumphalism or success; it may indeed be labeled failure. The history of ministry in the city is littered with the bodies of pastors who survived only a short time.

Yet if the church is serious about ministry in the great cities of our world, we must be prepared to train, equip, and send into city ministry pastors who will make a long-term commitment to stay there in spite of cultural shock, mounting crime rates, racial tensions, and the inadequacy of the social systems; to stay without much affirmation or support from the church-at-large, without enough salary to make ends meet, without golf club memberships, decent cars, dinners in fancy restaurants or Caribbean cruises! In other words, clowns.

The city simply invites the clown-pastor to penetrate its very heart, deliberately participating in its tragic realities and helping it in all seriousness to discover laughter and hope in the center of life.

At some point in history, says Floyd Shaffer, "the word *clown* was derived from the word *clod,* meaning 'one who is lowliest of the low, called upon to do work that others will not do.' "³ Shaffer believes that the word "clown" can be substituted for "servant" (the Greek word is *doulos* or slave) in many New Testament texts without violating the text. Both words describe persons who do work that others won't do because of its lowly character.⁴

Such a practice of ministry must be informed by the incarnation of our Lord. The "Grand Miracle" as C. S. Lewis calls the incarnation, is that God comes down, down *into* humanity. "But he goes down," says Lewis, "to bring the whole ruined world up with him."⁵ To follow the way of Jesus means giving up one's power, one's glory and taking upon one's self the "form of a slave."⁶ The very fact that someone, who might have enjoyed some of the privileges and benefits of our economic system, chooses instead to forsake these kinds of rewards in order to share a less attractive existence has, in itself, a transforming power. Is it too much to ask a disciple of Christ to demonstrate the kind of love that shares the same risks to which the people are exposed? Is it unrealistic to ask the servant to share the same kind of powerlessness the Master experienced?

Some of us who have worked with congregations in the cities of our land have asked that pastors who accept calls to those congregations live out in very practical ways the implications of the incarnation for ministry. We are suggesting that only pastors who are willing to make a long-term commitment to ministry in those places be called. A ten-year commitment would be the minimum; a lifetime would be better. City congregations have been considered career stepping-stones for too long. Young pastors have sometimes been told to stay a couple of years until something better comes along. (We realize, of course, that this has been all too tragically true for the small rural congregation, also, but since the rural congregation has traditionally had a more stable social environment, short pastorates have not been as destructive. However, the drastic changes occurring in rural areas may call for similar long-term commitments.)

No one denies that this is tough. The city missionary has little adventure, no glamour and is constantly on call. As one pastor said, "You get caught up in the bottomless pit of people's needs. You know the gospel is love, and you give so much of yourself, your money and your time away, that pretty soon there's nothing left. You love the sick and you end up sick and burned-out yourself."

But long-term commitment may just possibly create the kind of environment that Floyd Shaffer tells us his clowns try to create, "an environment by which the community and world around us are transformed by the grace of God. Just maybe we don't 'perform' religion but create an environment to transform people."[7] At that point in history when clowns saw that Jesus' entire ministry was one of transformation, says Shaffer, "they began to act out this concept."[8]

Given that primary commitment to this style of ministry, the next requirement follows naturally. The pastor must live among the people. Jesus did not do his ministry from some distant planet. He lived on this earth, in one particular place with a particular group of people. There can be no uninvolved clowns in the rodeo; there can be no commuting pastors in the city. Incarnation means that one shares the same life and living conditions as the people. Mission has always made that a requirement and the rules have not changed.

Jesus was subject to the ills that humans have always endured. Being human meant suffering the same hunger and thirst and discomfort that the disciples suffered. For the city pastor that means living in the same high-crime areas, breathing the same polluted air, fighting the same crowded streets and highways, waiting in the same long lines to get services, despairing over the same political discriminations that others experience. It means you can't ask for another "call" just because you don't like the living conditions where you are. The pastor is not called to get people out of the city, to move them into another social class, to get them more of this world's goodies, but to proclaim and to model that "the kingdom of God is among you!"

For one young pastor that has meant fighting and incurring the wrath of a city council determined to bring in legalized gambling; it has meant starting a farmer's market so the people of that community can have fresh produce at a price they can afford; it has meant lobbying for new low-cost housing across the street from the church building; it has meant being shot in the leg during an argument between two families when he was serving as a mediator; and it has meant being burglarized over two-dozen times and being held up at gunpoint on the street outside his home.

Instead of ruffle and wig of a circus clown, the pastor ministers with a loaf of bread under one arm and a bottle of wine in the other hand. The pastor brings a sacramental presence to the city, and by simply being there points to Jesus as a living reality. In his lifetime Jesus changed little, but he gave himself as a down payment for what was yet to come. The pastor who stays in the city, enduring its indignities, often changing so little, affirms that other reality which Jesus brought to this world, the power of a transforming love. Like Jesus, the clown brings laughter, life, and community where before there were only tears, the stench of death, and alienation.

Episcopal priest Robert Farrar Capon says that "in the long run, Christianity is not a religion. . . . It is the proclamation of the gospel that God has fixed up everything himself, and it is an invitation to believe that incredibly cheerful good news. . . ." That's what restores laughter to the world, says Capon, and not anything we can do to fix it up and make it more religious.[9]

The clown is everyone and no one. The clown deliberately loses identifying characteristics under white makeup, distorting paint, strange wigs, and oddball costumes. One cannot tell if the clown is male or female, young or old, of a particular race or nationality. When pastors in the city are able to identify with but also transcend a diversity of cultures, they call forth gifts that are already there.

All of the gifts needed to transform ministry in the city are waiting to be called forth. The clown touches each cheek with the red dot of clowning and persons experience the love that goes with it. Their own gifts are affirmed. They have seen the clown survive dozens of pratfalls and scores of clumsy accidents, and they have laughed at the bull lunging futilely at the rolling barrel. By comparison their gifts look pretty good. They are no longer the lowliest of the low; there is one among them who is willing to be lower and more foolish.

The pastor as clown is a call to the strength of weakness and to the power of foolishness. It is a call to the ministry of discipleship and to the apostolate of servanthood. We do not need any more pastors who take a city congregation because it's the only call they can get while they are waiting for something better to come along. The city needs pastors who are caught up by the hilarity of the gospel and who remember that the city of the cross and the empty tomb was the destination toward which Jesus journeyed.[10]

CHAPTER **11**

Directions for Mission
in Changing Urban Communities

Warren A. Sorteberg

Poverty has always been a part of life in the central city, but through-out the industrial period cities offered employment for unskilled workers in factories and shops. This allowed people to move upward economically. Until the 1970s urban centers offered jobs for unskilled persons, and these jobs in turn meant that some of the poor were able to enter the American middle class. With the decline of the industrial age and the beginning of the technological age, or the "information society,"[1] employment opportunities for unskilled workers have been reduced dramatically. A study published in 1979 by the Carter administration concluded that the American city no longer provides unskilled employment for new immigrants nor does it assimilate other cultures into the American mainstream.[2] Now there is not just poverty, but a permanent underclass which cannot participate in traditional patterns of upward mobility. The church must make a new commitment to address this complex problem.

The inner city has become a stagnant pool where the poor are caught, and from which they cannot escape even through hard work and dedication to the American dream. Factories have closed and will continue to close at an accelerating rate. Businesses and in-dustries that provided unskilled jobs have moved out of the inner city, relocating in areas that are inaccessible to the urban poor. The growth of employment opportunities in the city has almost exclu-sively been in the fields of service (which pays little) and high technology (which is unavailable to the uneducated). According to

111

sociologist William Julius Wilson of the University of Chicago, the significant social change in contemporary America is that "class has become more important than race in determining Black access to privilege and power." What has developed is a "Black underclass in a hopeless state of stagnation, falling further and further behind the rest of society."[3] Wilson depicts the significant alteration that has effected structural change in the economy, particularly with respect to central city employment.[4] The central city proportion of manufacturing jobs in the twelve largest metropolitan areas dropped from 66 percent in 1947 to less than 40 percent in 1970. This development particularly affected the black unskilled worker who, even though employed at minimum wage, was unable to support himself and his family and continued to slip deeper into debt and poverty. Lack of success in the labor market destroyed self-confidence and promoted feelings of resignation, which in turn led to the abandonment of a job search, temporarily for some and per-manently for others.[5] Wilson further argues that class rather than race has become the dominating factor in the lives of those who live in the central city. Since 1970 both urban poor whites and nonwhites have made little progress moving out of the ranks of the underclass. Wilson suggests that one-third of the entire black popu-lation remains in the underclass, but that whites, Hispanics and Native Americans in significant numbers are also victims of class subordination.[6] He concludes that the growing gap between the "haves" and "have nots" has greater consequences in the inner city today than race. Every major city in the country today has thousands and thousands of homeless persons. These persons are not only single adults but children and adults with families who have no place to live and no means of support.

In an article in *The Atlantic Monthly* entitled "The Origins of the Underclass,"[7] Nicholas Lemann reported on a study of the black ghetto on the south side of Chicago. He describes a dysfunctional society in which none of the traditional institutions (family, school, job market, or church) work. Lemann calls the situation a "complete social breakdown." The breakdown can be traced in part to the fact that middle-class blacks have migrated out of the city during the last twenty years. The exodus of these more affluent and better-educated blacks to the suburbs has left behind a community that is essentially unemployed, uneducated, and leaderless. The people who remain are unable to extricate themselves from the destructive consequences of underclass status.[8] Lemann contends that all efforts to deal with the situation have failed. Welfare and job training programs, schools and the war on poverty have failed. The population in urban low-income high-rise apartments is 75 percent poor; 65 percent are under twenty-one; and 80 percent are female-headed families. The high school dropout rate is 89 percent.[9] The only "institution" that functions is the drug culture, and it perpetuates crime and neighborhood gangs that victimize the inner-city community.

The development of this urban underclass is a harsh and unavoidable fact of life in urban centers during the last decades of the twentieth century. If the Christian church is to address the people of the inner city, it must be prepared to tell the gospel to this permanent underclass, a growing social group that may never make it into the mainstream of American economic life. The nation tries to ignore this reality. The federal government has declared the war on poverty to be over, implying perhaps that the struggle has been won. That is not the case; there simply has been a cease-fire and withdrawal.

Theologian Harvey Cox argues that the main stimulus for the renewal of Christianity will come from the bottom and from the edge, from those sectors of the Christian world that are on the margins of the modern liberal consensus.[10] Cox describes the ministry with the poor and the oppressed as "the resurrection of life" for the Christian church. It is precisely in these communities of oppressed people that the gospel comes alive as a power to liberate them from their shackles. The experience of the church in Latin America with the base Christian communities demonstrates how the renewal of the church comes about as the biblical message is applied to the real issues of poverty and oppression.[11] Here, Cox contends, is the opportunity for a new reformation, here on the periphery of culture and intellectual life. The call to minister to the poor, therefore, is an opportunity to reclaim the power of the gospel in the contemporary world.

Not Race but Multiculturality

The racial picture in the United States today is not simply a matter of black and white. While blacks predominate in many inner-city communities of this nation, there are more than twenty million Hispanics who live for the most part in urban areas. Their number is growing so rapidly that the Hispanic population may reach between thirty and forty million persons by 1999. Asians presently make up five million persons of the American population; they are growing through immigration. New waves of immigrants, both legal and undocumented, are changing the face of American society in general and urban centers in particular. Los Angeles, for example, now is the third largest Spanish-speaking city in the world after Mexico City and Madrid, Spain. The population of Los Angeles proper is nearly 75 percent nonwhite, with blacks, Asians, and Hispanics constituting the major groups in this ethnic mosaic. It also boasts the largest Native American population in the country.

More than simple pluralism, this racial and cultural mosaic represents a complex multicultural society. The melting pot is no longer melting. Races and language groups are retaining their cultures and primary languages in homes, businesses, churches, and neighborhoods. While there is some assimilation, the major thrust is to maintain ethnic identity. The futurist John Naisbitt writes that we have "learned to celebrate ethnic diversity with new languages, ethnic food, restaurants and layers of foreign cultures around us that fit into the multiple-option mood. This new openness enriches everyone."[12]

The modern inner city is not a monolithic ghetto but a multicultural mosaic in which dozens of ethnic groups are represented. Sixteen ethnic groups, for instance, have been identified in Philadelphia and four neighboring cities. These linguistic and cultural communities include 6,000 Vietnamese, 10,000 Chinese (including both Cantonese-speaking and Mandarin-speaking people), 2,000 Laotians, 240,000 Russian Jews, and 500 Thais. These groups are maintaining their culture and language, and they constitute what amounts to a global mission field in the center of an American urban complex.[13]

The pluralism of the inner city also consists of many kinds of subcultures. There are lesbian and gay communities, street people, night people, the theatre crowd, yuppies, the drug culture, the deinstitutionalized and so on. A comparison recently has been made between the church and the supermarket. Ten years ago a supermarket had 8,000 products and a meat counter that closed at 6 P.M. while the store closed at 10 P.M. Today a supermarket stocks 22,000 products and stays open 24 hours a day. It features sections for Asian, Spanish, salt-free, gourmet, and generic foods. Multilingual checkers service the customers, and the supermarket provides as many financial services as a local bank. The nearby church, however, probably still uses only English in its worship, and that service is held once weekly, Sunday at 11 A.M. The challenge to urban ministry is for the church to respond with a 24-hour operation with night and day staffs so that it can be used like hospitals, grocery stores, and police stations.[14]

Bishop and theologian Lesslie Newbigin served nearly forty years as a missionary in India. He has returned to England where he now serves as pastor in an urban church in Birmingham. He notes that the hermeneutical task in the orient was to apply the message of Christianity cross-culturally. Much to his surprise, he has found that the most difficult task for Christian missions in the industrial West is to speak the gospel message within modern Western culture. Since the Enlightenment, people have been increasingly free to follow individual preferences regarding personal conduct and beliefs. A secularized society has relegated the Christian faith to being merely one among many religions. Newbigin believes that modern secular culture is a pagan society, and that its paganism has actually been born out of its rejection of Christianity. He contends that Western culture, which could be labeled "free Christian paganism," is far more resistant to the gospel than any other culture in the world today. Cross-cultural missions have been familiar in the past with the application of the gospel to pre-Christian cultures, but the greater challenge in our time is applying the gospel to Western post-Christian paganism. This is the new missionary frontier.[15]

Newbigin continues by asserting that the place of the church in its mission to the world is not with the establishment but with the protesters. As Jesus was crucified outside the walls of the city, so the place of the Christian must always be outside the citadel of the cultural establishment and on the side of its victims.[16] The missionary encounter with our culture, therefore, must see our own culture through the eyes of Christians shaped by other cultures. Newbigin believes that the Western world must recognize that it cannot do without the other cultures of the world.[17] Cross-cultural evangelism is, therefore, a great challenge but also an opportunity for the church to renew itself as it comes to understand the Christian faith through the eyes, ears, and languages of other cultures.

One Mission

The missionary call of the church sounds forth from the great commission of Christ as recorded in St. Matthew to "Go therefore and make disciples of all nations, baptizing them in the name of the Father and of the Son and of the Holy Spirit, and teaching them to obey everything that I have commanded you" (Matt. 28:19-20). Those words define the singular mission of the church for all time. The gospel, however, must always be carried in some cultural container. The gospel is transmitted in a variety of these cultural containers and takes on the shape of the receptacle in which it is transmitted. Many Lutherans have received the gospel in the cultural containers of Germanic and Scandinavian heritages, but sometimes the holder is mistaken for the gospel itself. German chorales and Scandinavian piety are appropriate for the transmission of the gospel and so are the beat of the African drum and the smoke from the Indian sage ceremony. The cultural imperialism which has imposed forms of ethno-European Christianity upon other cultures must come to an end.

Serious thought must be given to the problem of contextualization, that is, the placing of the gospel in the total context of a culture at a particular moment and letting that culture shape its expression of faith and ministry. Central to the culture is language, which shapes the ways people perceive and cope with life. Certainly the beliefs, experiences, and practices that express the meaning of life affect religion. Those religious insights determine how the gospel of Christ is received and how the faith of the church is articulated.[18]

The one mission of the church must be advanced in the multi-cultural context of the inner city. To accomplish this, three elements of the ministry are fundamental.

Kerygma. Proclamation has been at the center of the church's ministry through twenty centuries. The *kerygma* is the message that God in Jesus Christ has come to liberate humanity from all that would destroy life, and that in Christ the kingdom of God has drawn near. Preaching, sacramental life, worship, teaching, and nurture should take shape within the context of the community and culture where urban ministry is located.

Koinonia. Inner-city residents are often isolated from neighbors and surrounding cultures. Fear may prevent friendly outreach to those who are around them. The plight of solo parents and fragmented families, worsened by poverty, often results in separation and loneliness in a crowded city. Genuine human community is a great gift of the Christian faith, and is desperately needed in urban America. The longing for human community, the search for caring people, is overwhelming in the inner city. *Koinonia,* or Christian fellowship, is the biblical term for that sharing, which knits people together in a single family, namely the body of Christ. *Koinonia* is more than a potluck supper. In one sense, it is a foretaste of the true community that is promised in the coming kingdom of God. True *koinonia* flows out from the gospel and is sustained through the sacramental life of the church. In Holy Baptism we are incorporated into Christ and become members one of another. In the Eucharist all share in the one cup and the one loaf. This fellowship of believers is the work of the Holy Spirit.

Diaconia. The urban congregation has often been mistaken for a social-service agency. The church in the inner city is bombarded by cries for assistance, and a sensitive church may respond with ministries that seek to alleviate hunger, to provide shelter and clothing, to educate, and to provide health care. The Greek word for service is *diaconia,* one of the three essential elements in the one mission of the church. It is an unusually important dimension of urban ministry, and calls for creativity and energy on the part of pastors and leadership as they unite with others in ministry to the needy of a community. The service aspect of the urban church's mission includes advocacy. Not only is the church called to bind up the wounds of people, but it is called to seek social justice by addressing the systemic causes of inequality and oppression.

Directions for Urban Ministry

The United States is becoming more and more urbanized, and a large percent of its population reside in communities of a million or more persons. The final decade of the twentieth century and the early part of the twenty-first century will be an era of increasing global urbanization. This urbanization will radically affect the styles and methods of worldwide Christian evangelization.[19]

Ethnic pluralism has always been an element in urban life, and the changes being effected today create a "cultural pluralism" which is more permanent than that of earlier immigrant groups. The church can no longer assume that the English language and Anglo patterns will ultimately predominate in the lives of these communities. Changes will be necessary in the way the Lutheran church worships. Liturgies and hymns need to accommodate other cultures in order to convey the gospel for those ethnic groups.

A major problem confronting the Lutheran church as it faces the challenges of urban ministry in the next decades is the question of leadership. Less than 2 percent of the Lutheran church consists of people of color or persons whose primary language is other than English. An even smaller percentage have entered the professional ministry of the church. The result is that, for the most part, white pastors have carried on the church's ministries in the inner city to other races and cultures. While a growing number of blacks, Hispanics, and Asians, both clergy and lay, are beginning to enter pastoral service in the church, the numbers are still too small to sustain self-determined cross-cultural ministry. Churchwide initiatives to enlist, educate, and deploy people of color and primary language other than English in the professional leadership of the church constitutes a major challenge in the decades ahead. Some studies have indicated that the difference between success and failure in Spanish-language ministries, for instance, depends first on leadership that comes from the community being served and second on autonomous ethnic congregations that do not depend upon an Anglo church hosting their ministry.[20] These factors should be kept in mind as new ministries are developed in ethnic/language groups.

The Evangelical Lutheran Church in America has set as a goal an increase of its membership among people of color and primary language other than English from under 2 percent in 1988 to 10 percent in 1998. This calls for an increase of just under 500,000 people in the first ten years of the ELCA's life. The goal translates into approximately 50,000 people per year being received into the baptized membership of the Lutheran church or about 1,000 new persons of color and language added per week for a period of ten years. This is a challenge for urban ministry. Meeting it will require specific strategies and the support and commitment of the whole church.

The history of urban ministry in the Lutheran Church in America and the American Lutheran Church during the past thirty years has taught a number of important lessons to the church. The Lutheran church has lost hundreds of urban congregations in central cities because lack of financial resources and leadership prevented these congregations from carrying on the ministry needed in their changing communities. An isolated urban congregation rarely survives to be an effective place of ministry in the inner city. Financial support from churchwide agencies has assisted some such congregations to remain in place. It is clear that urban congregations need to work together with other congregations and synodical and national church agencies in order to carry out a strategy for mission in the city.

A variety of urban strategies need to be employed in the various metropolitan areas of the United States. Those area strategies that assess the needs of the community and then determine the strategy of response by the Lutheran church are particularly important. A major benefit from such strategic planning is the discovery of the corporate mission of the church, carried out as a team effort with sister congregations and agencies in the same parish area. Urban ministry also can be done ecumenically where there is a common agreement upon purposes and goals on the part of the cooperating

church bodies. The strategies for church planning and urban evangelism teams of other denominations should be explored in order
to benefit from their experience. The day is long past when each
congregation is an island and each denomination works in isolation
from others.

For too long the overriding concern of urban mission among
Lutherans has been the simple survival of its older city congregations. A deliberate effort has been made to provide assistance for
a transition ministry when a congregation sought to change the focus
of its ministry from one ethnic population to another, which has
moved into the community surrounding the church building. Frequently the purpose of such transition was simply the survival of a
building or the perpetuation of a traditional ministry. This is no
longer sufficient. The overall strategy of the Lutheran church in
urban ministry must be more than a defensive effort to cut its losses.
There must be an offensive strategy to plant new ministries in the
inner city and carry out a churchwide strategy for evangelization.

A final challenge to Lutheran urban ministry is the economic
deprivation concentrated in inner-city neighborhoods across the land.
The emergence of an underclass trapped in perpetual poverty
provides an enormous challenge for the Lutheran church which,
increasingly, has become a church of middle-class and upper middle-
class persons. Lutherans generally are prospering under the market
economy of what is called democratic capitalism. Many others are
not. The question is whether and how we will deal with our responsibility to the urban poor of this nation. The Lutheran church
has the resources, including professional people and financial ca-
pabilities, to develop a strategy of mission outreach to the poor in
urban America.

Conclusion

The church of Jesus Christ is called to carry out the great commission
of our Lord to bring the gospel to every human being. The expanding
urban centers of our nation set before us a multicultural mission

field of great proportions. The call to this mission involves both pain and promise, but in the city the church can truly become the people of God, persons of many cultures united in witness and service and the praise of God, a foretaste of the promised heavenly city.

CHAPTER **12**

The Global Dimensions of the Urban Mission Task

James A. Bergquist

Urban ministry has long occupied a position of special concern within the Christian mission. Today, however, there is a heightened awareness of the global dimensions of urbanization. For Christian mission, the 1990s have not only become the decade of the poor, but the decade of the urban poor.

The purpose of this chapter is to describe global urbanization today, to trace some past Christian responses to the challenge of urban ministry, and finally to survey some contemporary Christian movements in urban mission.

The Realities of Global Urbanization

"Hell Is a City" is the title Paul Harrison gives to that section of his book *Inside the Third World* in which he describes the phenomenal urbanization now under way in Africa, Asia, and Latin America.[1] Harrison, like others, can recognize positive aspects of global urbanization. His section title, however, does capture the demographic expansion of cities, coupled with the growing tendency of cities to be communities of the poor. There are several angles from which to describe global urbanization.

The statistics of growth. First, the number of urban dwellers as compared to rural people continues to increase, with the most rapid rates of increase in the Third World. Up until 1975 most of the world's urban dwellers lived in more developed countries. Today the balance has shifted and by the year 2000 two-thirds of urban populations will be in the Third World. The following chart demonstrates the trends.[2]

*Urban Dwellers as Percentage of
the Total Populations*

	1900	1985	2000 (projected)
Africa	4.0	29.1	39.0
East Asia	6.0	34.8	42.0
Europe	38.0	73.5	77.0
Latin America	13.0	67.3	83.0
Northern America	44.0	81.0	86.0
South Asia	7.0	26.3	35.0
USSR	9.0	68.7	83.0
World (as whole)	14.4	42.9	50.5

This accelerating global urbanization, due to rural migration as well as rapid population growth, has resulted in the emergence of hundreds of cities of unprecedented size. David Barrett has classified three types of burgeoning cities.[3] (1) *"Megacities" with populations of 1 million or more.* Rome was the first and only megacity in antiquity, but after its demise it fell to a population of 19,000 by A.D. 1380. Until 1770 there were no megacities in the world. By 1900 there were 20, among them London and New York, and all in the West except Tokyo and Calcutta. By 1985 there were 276 megacities, with 433 projected by A.D. 2000, most of them Third World cities. (2) *"Supercities" with populations of 4 million or more.* In 1985 there were 38, with about 125 projected by 2000. (3) *"Supergiants" with populations of 10 million or more.* In 1985 there were 9, with 24 projected by 2000. Not only will the largest number of mega and supercities be in the Third World within our lifetime, but 21 of the 24 supergiants will be non-Western by A.D. 2000.

Urbanization and poverty. It is also clear that global urbanization has been accompanied by global poverty on an unprecedented scale. Jobs, food, housing, and public services are in short supply, often critically so. While Western cities are thinning out to the suburbs, leaving a culture of poverty in the inner cities, Third World cities are surrounded and penetrated by slums, shanties, bustees, and barrios. Paul Harrison has described Third World cities as small islands of affluence set in a sea of misery, surrounded by vast belts of poverty, "monstrous accretions of virtual ghettoes for the excluded and the unwashed."[4] Overall, the urban labor force of the Third World will grow by 60 percent by the year 2000 (by 103 percent in Latin America alone). The International Labor Organization estimates that two-fifths of the entire labor force is presently unemployed or underemployed, and that with the continued growth of population, including the cities, more than one billion new jobs have to be created in the Third World before the end of the century.

Why do people keep coming? Because as bad as conditions are in the cities, the rural conditions left behind are worse. "Migration, then," says Harrison, "is a form of voting with your feet, of demanding a seat at the table where the feasting is going on. It happens because development is uneven and the benefits of growth are so unevenly spread. It is a protest against inequality."[5] Thus the rural poor continue to migrate to the cities and live in places that are likely to consolidate and perpetuate their poverty. Harrison concludes: "But, ultimately, the only way of halting hyper-urbanization is by reducing the obscene gap between city and rural incomes, investing in improvements that will help keep the rural poor on the land. The problem of overblown cities, in other words, cannot be solved until the problem of underdeveloped rural areas is attacked."[6]

The size and poverty of the exploding Third World cities therefore make urban mission a top priority for Christians. Roger Greenway states the obvious but unassimilated consequence: "This is a field in which Christian economists, sociologists, politicians, business leaders, theologians, and missionaries should be engaged; thinking intensely, principally, and practically about the challenges of the city."[7]

Urbanization and secularization. In 1965, Harvey Cox viewed the processes of urbanization and secularization as a single and largely positive development marked by the collapse of traditional religions. Certainly urbanization and secularization are worldwide phenomena, not limited to the West, and certainly the patterns

124

of traditional rural piety are often broken in the cities of Africa and Asia as well as in the Western world. But secularity has penetrated rural as well as urban life. As Harvie Conn has argued in a recent article, secularization is not in fact identical with urbanization, neither in the West nor in the Third World. The true picture is more complicated. The reality of urban life is marked by both a growing secularism and loss of traditional faith as well as by evidence of vital new forms of religious expression, Christian and others. Conn warns against either idealizing secularism or heaping upon it the sole blame for the loss of faith, depersonalization, anarchy, and poverty often found in cities.[8] What is needed, in short, is a new form of missionary engagement in the cities.

A declining Christian presence proportionate to the population growth of the cities. Such missionary engagement is required because globally, as well as in the Western world, the numbers of baptized or affiliated church members of all confessions has declined markedly throughout the twentieth century as a proportion of urban populations. In 1900, 69 percent of all urban dwellers were Christian—reflecting the fact that most of the largest cities of the world were Western. By 1985 that proportion has dropped to 46 percent; by the year 2000 it may be less than 44 percent. Thus, writes David Barrett, from whose analyses these statistics were drawn, the churches "are fast losing the battle to disciple the cities."[9] Superiority of numbers by Christians will not in itself save the cities, but without effective Christian presence, participation, and witness, there will be no generating center for renewal.

The realities of global urbanization, we may conclude, are marked today by massive growth, a desperate human condition, and a declining Christian presence.

Many Christians find these urban realities demoralizing, problems in the category of what futurist Alvin Toffler terms "stymied issues"—polarized situations everybody dislikes but about which nobody seems to have a clue as to what to do.[10] Christian realism will reject simplistic solutions, the quick fixes of either massive evangelism campaigns and church planting strategies or secular programs of economic and political development. Both are needed. But what is needed most is a faith that perseveres in the long haul.

Clinton E. Stockwell points to the way of grace: "We may be as inconspicuous as salt on a plate of rice, but Jesus Christ calls us to preserve and provide the savour of city life, to bear witness to the promised New Jerusalem. We will be sustained not by success but by the salvation and abiding presence of Jesus himself. . . ."[11]

Urban Ministry in the History of Christian Mission

The Christian church was involved globally in urban mission from its beginnings. In the strict sense of the term, however, there was no specific urban mission until after the industrial revolution. In the late 1700s and early 1800s, mass movements of people toward the growing commercial and industrial urban centers commenced, first in Europe and America and somewhat later in the rest of the world, provoking the accelerating human displacements which prefigured those we face today. Once the process of urbanization began, Christians were not slow to respond to the new missionary challenges.

We may trace several distinct (but overlapping) stages in the development of urban mission, all of which have some enduring validity.

Discovering the urban poor: voluntarism and revival (1820–1875). As rural people were drawn to the factories and slums of the new industrial cities of Europe and America, the churches discovered the urban poor who crowded the tenements and were victimized by exploitative employment, crime, disease, and poverty.[12] The churches responded with methods characteristic of the times: voluntary societies and revival preaching.

Hundreds of mission societies were organized during the early 1800s. Many focused on foreign missions. But others were organized to deal with Western urban poverty—the Female Missionary Society for the Poor of the City of New York (1816), the Society for Employing the Poor (Boston 1820), the Association for the Improvement of the Condition of the Poor (New York 1944), the London City Mission (1832), and others.[13] The societies were mostly organized as voluntary associations of individuals, apart from denominational structures, were often lay led, and became the primary Protestant vehicle for urban mission during this period—the equivalent of the Roman Catholic missionary orders.

Revivalism informed the theological content of the mission societies. It also became the second chief vehicle of Protestant urban missions. Revivalism grew out of the two Great Awakenings of the 1740s and 1840s in America. By the mid-1800s it began to concentrate upon the cities, as, for example, in the work of Charles Finney in New York, Philadelphia, and Boston. Nineteenth-century revivalism emphasized personal conversion, but did not then neglect social reform. It brought considerable energy to both tasks in the city.

The Protestant movements of voluntarism and revival were limited in two ways. On the one hand, neither broke their individualist framework to deal with the underlying structural causes of poverty. Social reform was understood as changing individuals (poor and rich) and not as changing urban society. Eventually the movement was captured by status-quo business interests.[14] On the one hand, Protestant Christianity as a whole could not adequately cope with city ministry because of its inherent rural orientation, ethnic particularism, and individualism. Especially in the United States, Protestants found it difficult to plan comprehensively for ministry in a given urban area marked by poverty and cultural pluralism.[15]

As Latourette has remarked, Protestants did not totally fail but displayed considerable initiative, imagination, and intelligence with respect to urban mission.[16] Nevertheless, the rise of industrial cities in the nineteenth century was marked in Europe by extensive alienation of the working classes from the churches, and in America by an inability to adapt patterns suitable for rural ministry to urban mission. The struggle for effective urban mission is as old as the modern city itself.

Discovering the structures of urban poverty: the social gospel movement (1875–1920). After the Civil War a significant change took place in the understanding of urban poverty. Due in large part to the rise of labor movements and the development of social sciences, attention shifted from the problems of the poor to the underlying economic and social causes of poverty. Urban mission was

deeply influenced by the social gospel movement.[17] It is not sur-
prising that the first leaders of this movement in the United States
were urban church people who saw what was happening in their
cities. Washington Gladden, minister of North Congregational
Church in Springfield, Massachusetts, began his prolific speaking
and writing career in 1875 as he faced the social injustices of his
community. Ronald C. White, Jr., writes that "the experience of
Washington Gladden was repeated again and again in other settings;
ministers and laypersons, nurtured in an evangelical religion that
emphasized individual salvation, confronted with a new world born
of the industrial revolution, were forced to rethink their whole understanding of Christian faith and life."[18] Walter Rauschenbush, a
Baptist parish pastor in New York, discovered that Hell's Kitchen
"was not a safe place for saved souls."[19]

Although the social gospel movement may be faulted for its
overly optimistic identification of the kingdom of God with a just
human society, it did have a positive effect on urban mission. It
focused attention on systems as well as individuals (predating one
theme of liberation theology by more than half a century). It rightly
called for social action as well as compassion and service. And it
deeply influenced subsequent twentieth-century movements for
global mission with its emphasis upon social justice.

Discovering global urban mission (1920–1980). One of the
first attempts to rethink Christian mission in terms of a newly emerging global urban reality took shape at the 1928 meeting in Jerusalem
of the International Missionary Council. That council adopted a
statement titled "The Christian Mission in Relation to Industrial
Problems in Asia and Africa."[20] The statement helped provide the
climate within which a great many urban-industrial missions developed and flourished worldwide up to and after World War II.
Under the influence of Barthian and other neoorthodox theologies,
the International Missionary Council itself rejected the Jerusalem
statements. Yet directions were established from which there was
no turning back: urban mission involved both personal salvation and
corporate social action. Though the proper relationship of these two
components continued to be debated, there was wide agreement that
industrial mission required high priority.

128

James A. Bergquist

After World War II, secularization and its part in the urbanization process came to the fore. It was clear by then that secularization, like urbanization, was a global process. Estimates of whether secularization was a promise or a threat varied greatly. Harvey Cox's *The Secular City* provided a largely positive assessment of secularity as a turning away from other worlds to this one.[21] Gibson Winter, in his *The New Creation as Metropolis,* was critical of the failure of the social gospel to discriminate between the kingdom of God and a just society, but he recognized in the metropolis the possibility of a unified human society arising out of the chaos of massive urban areas. Believing the traditional parish model to be inadequate, he called for new forms of church life in which Christians could live as secular servants and prophetic communities in the cities.[22] Meanwhile, Jacques Ellul in *The Meaning of the City* judged the city in largely negative terms as the center of human rebellion against God, a sign of the substitution of dehumanizing and godless technology for God's creation. He held out the hope of God's redemption of the city, but only beyond history.[23]

The idea of a global urban mission centered strongly on participation in the secular processes of revolutionary change became at least partially institutionalized in the World Council of Churches during the 1960s, especially in connection with the Uppsala Assembly of 1968. Within the Protestant ecumenical movement "humanization and salvation" became a central motif, "rapid social change" emerged as a programmatic emphasis, and "the world sets the agenda" served as the watchword for evangelization. Out of the milieu, represented by these clusters of ideas, grew a number of urban mission training programs in the United States and in cities around the world.

The rapid social change movement was not without its critics. From outside the ecumenical movement, Donald McGavran's church growth approach developed in some measure as a protest against what he thought to be the near total neglect of conversion and personal salvation within the missiology of the ecumenical movement.[24] The church growth movement helped rally evangelicals around the world to renewed efforts to rethink and develop new strategies for urban evangelism.[25] From inside the ecumenical movement, the veteran missiologist Bishop Lesslie Newbigin sustained his criticisms of what he perceived to be the secular humanist presuppositions of the rapid social-change movement. He did so on the basis of a Trinitarian theology of mission in his *The Open Secret* (1978) and many earlier writings. While fully accepting the need for a missionary engagement with unjust social structures, he also continued to insist that urban and other missions had to deal with conversion and personal salvation. In this area he preferred the work of Roland Allen to that of Donald McGavran.[26]

It should also be noted that Lutherans in the United States during the 1950s and 1960s produced a number of research studies and programs on urban mission, most done under the cooperative umbrella of the Division of American Missions of the National Lutheran Council. The work of Walter Kloetzli especially must be mentioned for its confessional orientation, its use of interdisciplinary resources, commitment to both the personal and corporate dimensions of mission, and practical assistance to the churches.[27] The community action legacy of Saul Alinsky also influenced a number of parish-based community action ministries from the late 1960s to the present.[28]

The explosion of various liberation theologies in the global Christian consciousness from the 1970s until now have become dominant forces in shaping Roman Catholic, mainline protestant, and even conservative evangelical understandings of urban mission.[29] Liberation theology has deepened the older social gospel critique of the structural causes of injustice by analyzing those root causes within the context of today's postcolonial world. And with its own strong emphases upon the base church and people's participation in their own liberation, liberation theology has offered an alternative to the voluntary lay participation typical of nineteenth-century Evangelicals.

Challenging the Global Urban Frontier Today

The mainline Protestant and Lutheran traditions are not at the forefront of urban ministry in its global dimensions. There are no movements among them approaching the vigor of the voluntary societies of the early 1800s or reflecting the passion for the cities and theological intensity of the social gospel movement in the early 1900s. Even the community action based programs of the 1960s and 1970s seem to have reached a dead end, though many individual denominations in this country are continuing forward through somewhat isolated programs of various missions units.

Where is there focused attention on global urban ministry today? The most visible, informed, and comprehensive reflection is being offered by the Evangelical movement. Much of its focus is global and involves effective partnership with Third World Christians. Research is being done; strategies are being debated and planned; leaders are being trained; theological study is taking place that has incorporated and gone beyond the personal salvation/structural change debate. We should note the wide range of publications generated by Evangelicals—books, studies, and periodicals that are carefully done, comprehensive in theological outlook, and informed by the social sciences.[30] The journal *Urban Mission* has been published since 1983 by Westminster Seminary, designed apparently to provide a balanced diet of articles, research (biblical, theological, sociological), and practical case studies. In its editor and on its pages we meet the authors producing today's books on urban mission—Roger Greenway, Harvie Conn, Raymond Bakke, Clinton Stockwell, Luther Copeland, and others, all tirelessly holding up urban ministry in its global dimensions.

The best single document analyzing worldwide urbanization is David B. Barrett's *World-Class Cities and World Evangelization.*[31] In under sixty pages Barrett has produced a narrative loaded with statistics, graphs, chronologies, and scales projecting the growth of cities to the year A.D. 2025, tracing the effect upon Christian mission, and suggesting global evangelism for cities. The study was commissioned by the Southern Baptists who engaged the services of Barrett, a British Anglican, one of the most influential and prolific researchers in missiology today.

Another document which serves as a model for serious planning for urban mission is the 1985 report of the Archbishop of Canterbury's Commission on Urban Priority Areas.[32] Titled *Faith in the City: A Call for Action by Church and Nation,* its recommendations have stirred interest within the churches of Great Britain and even political controversy throughout the nation.

While it is impossible to do more than recall the current Roman Catholic contributions to global urban mission, one book deserves some attention. It is Benjamin Tonna's *Gospel for the Cities.*[33] A native of Malta, a priest, sociologist, and missiologist, Tonna has produced a study of unique value. He offers solid social and historical analysis combined with the best of post-Vatican II Roman Catholic biblical and missiological insights. The first part of his book deals with the historical process of urbanization, and the second with the Third World and urban mission. Especially helpful are his chapters on "Solidarity as Generic Mission," "Evangelization as Specific Mission," and "The Church as Mission."

Urban mission is nothing less than an invitation to participate in Christ's own mission. It is therefore first of all a gift and not a task. Yet responsible participation will require the best we have to offer. We can affirm with David Barrett: "When we remember that the wildfire expansion of Christianity in the first four centuries after Christ took place largely as an urban phenomenon assisted by the presence of the great cities of the Roman Empire, it should be possible for something similar to take place in the near and distant future, if only one would recover the early Christian's vision and zeal."[34]

Appendix: The Parish as Place: Principles of Parish Ministry

Harvey S. Peters, Jr.

This paper is written in the hope that pastors and lay members of the Lutheran church would be helped to understand more clearly their calling to do ministry in, with, and for a particular place. It is an attempt to integrate what it means to manifest Jesus Christ and to participate in the circumstances of all of the people in each place.

This paper avoids speaking of models of ministry that can, presumably, be replicated or transferred from one place to another. Instead, certain principles are identified that can be applied in every place, allowing for the distinctive form most appropriate for particular times and conditions. As a general premise, the mission of God is a given. This paper indicates that the ministry of the church, as it participates in God's mission, should be shaped by the circumstances for each time and place.

This paper was used to inform pastors and lay members of the Lutheran church regarding the stance in ministry that was supported and advocated by the Division for Mission in North America of the former Lutheran Church in America and the Division for Service and Mission of the former American Lutheran Church.

It should be noted that this stance in ministry required the interpretation and support of all parts of the church. Where it had "taken," there was clear evidence of strong leadership on the part of the synodical/district bishop who stated these principles and expects them to be applied. Conversely, money and rhetoric alone did not make them a reality without a consistent commitment on the part of the leaders in the church at all points. The teaching of this

understanding of ministry had to take place in seminaries, intern-
ships, the council of bishops, and their staffs—in addition to the
day-to-day work of parish ministry.

The reader should be aware that these principles have emerged
out of the experience of many pastors and congregations as they
have found changing circumstances in urban and rural areas. All
can profit by their experience and the examination of the biblical
foundations that have informed this understanding of ministry.

Biblical and Historical Background

The church's ministry is rooted in God's Word. The church's ministry
is informed and shaped by circumstances in God's world. Ministry
is the activity of God's people, the church, participating in God's
mission in and for the world.

The following paragraph is a concise summary of truths proclaimed through the testimony of our forebears. It describes the
purposes of God as the one who creates all that is and buys it back.
The world and all who dwell therein are the object of God's mission.

God, the very one who existed before all else, in Jesus, entered
the world, lived in it as a sojourner, and so fully identified with the
circumstances of humanity as to become a human. In that way God
took on the enemies of the good creation—sin, death, and evil in
all of their expressions—and succumbed to their power in order to
break their hold on all those who inhabit that place. In doing so,
Jesus the Christ became the firstborn of a new creation—a new
citizen of a new realm. The church, the community of baptized who
have been called, gathered and empowered by the Holy Spirit, is
to embody this ministry of Christ in each time and every place as
a sign of the new creation.

It is not possible to speak of the church's ministry apart from
its purpose for and relationship to a specific place any more than it
would be possible to speak of Jesus' ministry without speaking of
Jerusalem. The church *in* each place is the church *for* that place.
Just as God chose Israel to be a blessing for all nations and just as
God appeared in human form for the sake of the world, so the church

exists not for itself but for every hamlet, town, neighborhood, barrio, hollow, country, city, and person.

Currently within the Lutheran church in the United States and in the Caribbean there is a growing need to rediscover the relationship between the ministry of each congregation and the place in which it is located.

While that relationship may be described demographically, sociologically, or historically, this is basically a theological concern. What is the object of each congregation's ministry if it is to be a faithful incarnation of the ministry of Jesus? How can the church be helped to rediscover what it means to be responsible for bearing Christ's ministry to its place?

Perhaps such a rediscovery can begin with understanding the difference between the words "congregation" and "parish." These words are often used interchangeably, thereby revealing the confusion that exists regarding for whom God's mission is intended.

The Bible has a word for this understanding of the creation as the object of God's salvation and justice. In Greek, it is *oikoumene*. This translates, "the whole inhabited earth, the world." In the Greek translation of the psalm, we read, "The Earth is the Lord's and the fulness thereof, the *oikoumene* and they that dwell therein."

In the New Testament we read in Luke's Gospel of Jesus being tempted when "the devil took him up and showed him all the kingdoms of the *oikoumene*." In Matthew's Gospel, the words of Jesus to his disciples about the last days speak of "this gospel of the kingdom will be preached throughout the whole *oikoumene*, as a testimony to all nations and then the end will come."

Originally the meaning was "the inhabited creation." Over the centuries this understanding has changed to the point that the word "ecumenical" has come to refer to relationships within the church. There are historical reasons for this, especially as the church took on the "indelible impress of the political framework" of the Roman Empire. During the ensuing centuries the distinctive nature of the *ekklesia* (church) and the *oikoumene* (inhabited creation) became fused and confused.

The word parish has had an equally interesting evolution. It derives from two Greek words, *para oike*, meaning "dwelling near, neighboring." It is the stance that a congregation takes in a particular place (parish) when it seeks to incarnate the ministry of Jesus. In the New Testament a "parochial" person is one who lives in a place without the right of citizenship—a sojourner like Jesus. Using the words of Paul, one who is "in but not of" the world. It will serve the church well if the meaning of parish as the "inhabited place" in which the congregation is called to incarnate the ministry of Jesus can be rediscovered.

A congregation is an expression of the church (*ekklesia*). A parish is an expression of the inhabited creation (*oikoumene*). A congregation exists for its parish just as the church exists for the world. A congregation that does not make this distinction clearly runs the risk of seeing its existence as an end in itself—with members spending most, if not all, of their energies to serve one another exclusively rather than ministering to the people in their parish.

Over the past two decades a concerted effort by the Lutheran church to recapture the understanding of the parish as place has resulted in significant renewal of ministry. What follows are fundamental principles of parish ministry that have been rediscovered by experience. They can be applied by any congregation that desires to have its ministry rooted or rerooted in its parish.

Principles of Parish Ministry

1. Parish ministry demonstrates the fullness of God's mission.
   • The ministry of the congregation is centered in the means of grace exclusively to the church—the Word and the sacraments of Baptism and the Eucharist.
   • The congregation strives to incarnate the ministry of Christ through its programs and to participate in God's continuing creation through its involvement in the life of the parish.
   • Seen collectively, the ministry of the congregation to the parish demonstrates the proclamation of God's love for the parish and actions that work for just conditions for all who inhabit that place.
   • The congregation and the pastor consciously seek to incarnate the presence of Christ in the parish by identifying with hopes and struggles of the poor and those who have been marginalized.

2. Parish ministry is geographical and integral to its setting.
• The pastor lives in the parish. The members of the congregation increasingly reside in the parish. They know their neighbors and are directly involved in the institutions of that place.
• The pastor and the congregation are consciously aware of their ministry as a sign, foretaste, and instrument of God's kingdom in relation to the realities of their parish.
• The pastor and the congregation demonstrate in their worship as well as in their public ministries a sense of responsibility and respect for the welfare of all people in the parish.
• The pastor and the congregation participate with others in the parish in community organizations that seek justice and promote well-being for all of the citizens.
• The pastor and the congregation are visible and known by name among others in the parish.
• The pastor and the congregation welcome others not living in the parish and who desire to be a part of the fellowship and ministry of the congregation in this place.

3. Parish ministry is inclusive.
• The congregation's membership increasingly reflects the racial economic, cultural, and social composition of the people in the parish.
• The pastor and the congregation actively welcome and celebrate the gifts of racial, ethnic, and cultural diversity that come from an inclusive ministry.
• The liturgies of the congregation and other aspects of the congregation's life use the languages and varied cultural traditions of the people from the parish.
• The pastor is assisted and supported by the congregation in becoming equipped to minister in a multicultural setting when the parish reflects this need.

4. Parish ministry is interdependent.
• The pastor and the congregation are fully involved in a relationship of mutual support and accountability with other ministries of the Lutheran church in the area.
• The pastor and the congregation engage in ministry for their parish consciously representing the entire Lutheran church and are aware of its support at all levels.

• The pastor, as the primary teacher in the congregation, meets regularly with other pastors for study, prayer, consolation, and mutual support.

5. Parish ministry is catholic.

• The pastor and the congregation understand that they share the responsibility of ministry in and for their parish with all other congregations of the one holy catholic apostolic church that are located in the same parish.

• The pastor and the congregation actively seek ways they can demonstrate the unity of the church as together with other congregations they seek to witness to God's saving love in Jesus Christ and to serve and advocate justice for the parish they share.

• Special emphasis is given by the various congregations of the church to efforts that result in empowerment of people for mutual determination about community life within the parish. The church, as one among many institutions in that place, demonstrates its solidarity with the oppressed in that parish in ways that will benefit all.

6. Parish ministry is intentional.

• The pastor makes repeated calls in the homes of parishioners, inviting them to unite in the life and ministry of the congregation. Members of the congregation assist in this effort.

• The pastor and the congregation avoid the development of a "clientele" by assuring that all programs include an invitation into the full blessings of membership in the fellowship of the church and the means of grace.

• The synod/district and churchwide agencies and other local ministries of the Lutheran church make their decisions with respect to how those decisions will affect the ministry of others. Decisions regarding funding, placement of pastors, interns, and other staff should be intentional and informed by the circumstances of the parish.

For additional reading on this subject:

Latourette, Kenneth Scott. *A History of Christianity.* New York: Harper & Brothers, 1963.

McCurley, Foster R. *Ancient Myths and Biblical Faith: Scriptural Transformations.* Philadelphia: Fortress Press, 1983.

Newbigin, Lesslie. "What is 'A Local Church Truly United'?" *Ecumenical Review,* Vol. 29, 1977.

Simmons, Gordon, "This Is Our Turf." Northwest Philadelphia Lutheran Parish, 1984.

Sinnott, Thomas. "Parish Calling: Theology, Typology, and Tips." South Hudson Evangelical Lutheran Parish, 1985.

Visser 'T Hooft, W. A. "The Meaning of Ecumenical." *The Burge Memorial Lecture.* London: SCM Press, 1953.

Notes

Chapter 4: Welcoming the Stranger

1. Roland H. Bainton, *The Martin Luther Easter Book* (Philadelphia: Fortress Press, 1983), 78.
2. Ibid., 78.
3. John Koenig, *New Testament Hospitality: Partnership with Strangers as Promise and Mission* (Philadelphia: Fortress Press, 1985).
4. Ibid., 5.
5. Ibid., 16.
6. Thomas W. Ogletree, *Hospitality to the Stranger: Dimensions of Moral Understanding* (Philadelphia: Fortress Press, 1985), 2–3.
7. Gustavo Gutierrez, *The Power of the Poor in History* (Maryknoll, N.Y.: Orbis Books, 1983).
8. Ibid., viii.
9. Ibid., 57.
10. Koenig, *New Testament Hospitality,* 146.
11. Williston Walker, Richard Norris, David W. Lotz, Robert T. Handy, *A History of the Christian Church,* 4th ed. (New York: Charles Scribner's Sons, 1985), 23–24.
12. Thomas W. Ogletree, *Hospitality to the Stranger,* 4.
13. Frederick W. Danker, *Jesus and the New Age* (St. Louis, Mo.: Clayton Publishing House, 1972), 250.

Chapter 10: The Clown: An Image of Hope from the Church in the City

1. *Los Angeles Times,* 30 March 1985, Vol. CIV, No. 117, E17.
2. Frederick Buechner, *Telling the Truth* (New York: Harper & Row, 1977), 60.
3. Floyd Shaffer, *If I Were a Clown* (Minneapolis: Augsburg Publishing House, 1984), 16.
4. Ibid., 78–79.
5. C. S. Lewis, *Miracles* (New York: Macmillan Co., 1978), 111.
6. Phil. 2:7.
7. Shaffer, *If I Were a Clown,* 54.
8. Ibid., 52.

9. Robert Farrar Capon, "The Uselessness of Religion," *Christianity Today,* 7 September 1984, 54.
10. This presentation is adapted from the C. C. Hein Lectureship delivered at the seminaries of the former American Lutheran Church.

Chapter 11: Directions for Mission in Changing Urban Communities

1. John Naisbitt, *Megatrends* (New York: Warner Books, 1982), 1.
2. *Urban America in the Eighties,* U.S. Government Printing Office, Washington, D.C.
3. William Julius Wilson, *The Declining Significance of Race* (Chicago: University of Chicago Press, 1978), 2.
4. Ibid., 93.
5. Ibid., 107.
6. Ibid., 154.
7. Nicholas Lemann, "The Origins of the Underclass," *The Atlantic Monthly,* June and July 1986, 32ff.
8. Ibid., 53.
9. Ibid., 55.
10. Harvey Cox, *Religion in the Secular City* (New York: Simon & Schuster, 1984), 208.
11. Ibid., 209.
12. Naisbitt, *Megatrends,* 283.
13. Roger Greenway, "Who Lives in This City?" *Urban Mission,* May 1986, 57.
14. Raymond Bakke, "The Challenge of World Urbanization to Mission Strategy," *Urban Mission,* September 1986, 12.
15. Lesslie Newbigin, *Foolishness to the Greeks* (Grand Rapids: Wm. B. Eerdmans, 1986), 20.
16. Ibid., 125.
17. Ibid., 148.
18. Ibid., 3.
19. Frank Allen, "Toward a Biblical Urban Mission," *Urban Mission,* January 1986.
20. Dan Long, "Some Serious Talk about Inclusive Ministry," Division for Service and Mission, The American Lutheran Church, 1986 (mimeographed report).

Chapter 12: The Global Dimensions of the Urban Missions Task

1. Paul Harrison, *Inside the Third World* (Harmondsworth, England: Penguin Books, 1979, rev. 1982), 139–210.
2. Adapted from material presented by David B. Barrett, editor, in *World Christian Encyclopedia: A Comparative Study of Churches and Religions in the Modern World A.D. 1900-2000* (London: Oxford University Press, 1982), 780.
3. David B. Barrett, *World-Class Cities and World Evangelization* (Birmingham, Ala.: New Hope, 1986), 21, and Appendix C, 48–49.
4. Harrison, *Inside the Third World,* 160.

5. Ibid., 149.
6. Ibid., 175.
7. Roger S. Greenway, "Content and Context: The Whole Christ for the Whole City," *Discipling the City*, ed. Roger S. Greenway (Grand Rapids: Baker Book House, 1979), 88.
8. Harvie M. Conn, "Any Faith Dies in the City," *Urban Mission* (May 1986), 6–19.
9. Barrett, *World-Class Cities and World Evangelization*, p. 11 and Chart 10, p. 15.
10. Alvin Toffler, "Here Comes the Future," *Grapevine: Joint Action and Strategy Committee* (October 1986), 4.
11. Clinton E. Stockwell in the Preface to *The Gospel and Urbanization* (Ventnor, N.J.: Overseas Ministries Study Center, 1985), 9.
12. Ronald C. White, "Social Reform and the Social Gospel in America," *Separation without Hope,* ed. Julio de Santa Ana (Maryknoll, N.Y.: Orbis Books, 1979), 50–52. For a novel that vividly portrays these conditions in London, see Michael Crichton, *The Great Train Robbery.*
13. White, *Separation,* 51. See also Wilbur C. Hallenback, *Urban Organization of Protestantism* (New York: Harper & Brothers, 1934).
14. Harvie M. Conn, "The Kingdom of God and the City of Man: A History of the City/Church Dialogue" in *Discipling the City,* 36: "Unaware of the ideology of the secularist religion of the megalopolis, the evangelical increasingly identified himself and the gospel with status-quo capitalism and did not offer the city a Christian alternative to the social and political structures it had created."
15. Kenneth Scott Latourette, *A History of the Expansion of Christianity,* vol. 4, *The Great Century: Europe and the United States 1800–1914* (New York: Harper & Row, 1941, reissued by Grand Rapids: Zondervan, 1970), 368–69. He notes that the Roman Catholics and Orthodox had better results in urban ministry in the United States because of their ability to hold immigrants, most of whom settled in the cities, and because of their more centrally directed episcopal structures.
16. Latourette, *A History of Christianity,* 369–70.
17. White, *Separation,* 54–56 traces this story. For a longer treatment, see Ronald C. White, Jr. and C. Howard Hopkins, *The Social Gospel, Religion and Reform in Changing America* (Philadelphia: Temple University Press, 1976).
18. Ibid., 54.
19. Quoted by White, Ibid., 55.
20. *Christianity and the Growth of Industrialism in Asia, Africa and South America.* vol. 5, Report of the Jerusalem Meeting of the International Missionary Council (London: Oxford University Press, 1928), 181–94.
21. Harvey Cox, *The Secular City* (New York: Macmillan Co., 1965).
22. Gibson Winter, *The New Creation as Metropolis* (New York: Macmillan Co., 1963), 11. Winter defines metropolis not just as the city, but the form of the new emerging society characterized by networks of exploitative communities, competition, class and racial divisions. For the church to find its vocation in

this setting, Winter argues that it must recover involvement with the centers of power in the metropolis through the servanthood of the laity, a new form of the church. He finds the individualistic culture of traditional residential Protestant churches antithetical to today's need for cultivating ministry in public centers of responsibility.

23. Jacques Ellul, *The Meaning of the City* (Grand Rapids: Wm. B. Eerdmans, 1970).
24. Donald McGavran, ed., *The Conciliar-Evangelical Debate: The Crucial Documents 1964–1976* (Pasadena: William Carey Library, 1977).
25. As one example of Evangelical focus on the issue, see *Christian Witness to Large Cities*. Lausanne Occasional Paper no. 9 (Wheaton, Ill.: Lausanne Committee for World Evangelization, 1980).
26. Lesslie Newbigin, *The Open Secret* (Grand Rapids: Wm. B. Eerdmans, 1978). See also his personal reflections in the "Rapid Social Change" movement in his *Unfinished Agenda: An Autobiography* (Geneva: WCC Publications, 1985), 197. There, among other points, he comments "that 'Rapid Social Change' thinking has not developed any coherent theology and is in danger of identifying the movement of revolution with the work of redemption."
27. See the following books by Walter Kloetzli: *Challenge and Response in the City* (Rock Island, Ill.: Augustana Press, 1962); *The Church and the Urban Challenge* (Philadelphia: Muhlenberg Press, 1961); *The City Church: Death or Renewal* (Philadelphia: Muhlenberg Press, 1961); and with Arthur Hillman, *Urban Church Planning: The Church Discovers Its Community* (Philadelphia: Muhlenberg Press, 1958).
28. As related for example by a contemporary Lutheran urban pastor, Stephen P. Bouman, "Your Face, Your Cloak, Your Coat, Your Shoes: Parish-Based Community Organization" in *Urban Mission* (March 1986), 5-18.
29. The point is true not only of Latin American theologies of liberation, but also, for example, of the *"Minjung"* (people's) theology of Korea.
30. The most comprehensive bibliography on global urban mission was compiled by Clinton E. Stockwell for the 1985 seminar on the topic. It is published as a part of the workbook developed for the seminar titled *The Gospel and Urbanization,* 83–88. Five titles are representative of the emerging comprehensive Evangelical effort. (1) *Christian Witness to the Urban Poor.* Lausanne Occasional Paper no. 22 (Wheaton, Ill.: Lausanne Committee for World Evangelization, 1980). (2) David Claerbaug, *Urban Ministry* (Grand Rapids: Zondervan, 1983). (3) Francis M. Dubose, *How Churches Grow in an Urban World* (Nashville: Broadman Press, 1978). (4) Roger S. Greenway, *Apostles to the City: Biblical Strategies for Urban Missions* (Grand Rapids: Baker Book House, 1978). (5) David J. Frenchak and Clinton E. Stockwell, comps. and Helen Ujvarosy, ed., *Signs of the Kingdom in the Secular City* (Chicago: Covenant Press, 1984).
31. Barrett, *World-Class Cities and World Evangelization.*

32. *Faith in the City: A Call for Action by Church and Nation.* The Report of the Archbishop of Canterbury's Commission on Urban Priority Areas (London: Church House Publishing, 1985). There is also a short, popular version of this 400-page study available.
33. Benjamin Tonna, *Gospel for the Cities,* trans. William E. Jerman, ATA (Maryknoll, N.Y.: Orbis Books, 1985).
34. Barrett, *World-Class Cities and World Evangelization,* 22.